Dance With Me

A Hopeful Romantic Interprets Ephesians 5

Dr. Debi Smith

Dream Dance Books

Newport Beach, California

Dance With Me
A Hopeful Romantic Interprets Ephesians 5
by Dr. Debi Smith

For information address:
    Dr. Debi Smith
    PO Box 13154
    Newport Beach, CA 92658
    www.DrDebiSmith.com

ISBN: 978-0-9885934-0-4

Printed in the United States of America

Ephesians 5:21-33

Submit to one another out of reverence for Christ.

Wives, submit yourselves to your own husbands as you do to the Lord. For the husband is the head of the wife as Christ is the head of the church, his body, of which he is the Savior. Now as the church submits to Christ, so also wives should submit to their husbands in everything.

Husbands, love your wives, just as Christ loved the church and gave himself up for her to make her holy, cleansing her by the washing with water through the word, and to present her to himself as a radiant church, without stain or wrinkle or any other blemish, but holy and blameless. In this same way, husbands ought to love their wives as their own bodies. He who loves his wife loves himself. After all, no one ever hated their own body, but they feed and care for their body, just as Christ does the church – for we are members of his body.

"For this reason a man will leave his father and mother and be united to his wife, and the two will become one flesh." This is a profound mystery – but I am talking about Christ and the church. However, each one of you also must love his wife as he loves himself, and the wife must respect her husband.

Acknowledgments

My life – and therefore this book – would not be possible without my parents. Thank you for giving me life, and for teaching me valuable lessons about its complexity, as well as its brevity. I promise to hold each day dear because of you, and to work diligently to become the best mom and gramma I can possibly be.

Thanks to my three sons for inspiring me to learn about men, and for being very patient with me in the process. I promise to keep learning.

I'm also grateful to the many psychologists, researchers, pastors, and faithful friends who have helped expand my understanding of men, life, and relationships: Jared, Dan, Stacia, Russ, Doug, Arvin, Joan, John, Gary, Keith, Scott, Jodi, Jennifer, Brian, Bill, Jim, Brent, Susan, Eric, and Ylena. I promise to remember the steps you taught me ... but I may need you to walk me through it just one more time.

Many thanks to all the men and women who have shared and processed their struggles with one another during our counseling sessions. You are the bravest people on this earth ... and the reason I do what I do. I promise to keep listening and learning from you.

... and to my Lord and Savior for making my path straight, though my faltering steps have often seemed random. Thanks for allowing me to see a glimpse of Your Hand at work in my life from time to time. I promise to hold on tight and to do the best I can for You.

And last, but by no means least, I want to express my very special appreciation to my dear friend, the one and only, totally amazing Fred Judkins. Thanks for dancing with me! You're the absolute best. And I promise to never give up.

Preface

Part 1: Dance With Me

Part 2: Just Follow My Lead

Part 3: Do You Love Me?

Part 4: The Sweethearts Ball

 *Preface*

LIFE'S A DANCE

There's a country song for everything. And just a little over a year ago, I took to heart the words of one in particular, beautifully sung by artist John Michael Montgomery:

> When I was 14 I was fallin' fast
> For a blue-eyed girl in my homeroom class
> Tryin' to get the courage to ask her out
> Was like tryin' to get oil from a water spout
>
> What she'd have said I can't say
> I never did ask and she moved away
> But I learned something from a blue-eyed girl
> Sink or swim you gotta give it a whirl
>
> Life's a Dance you learn as you go
> Sometimes you lead, sometimes you follow
> Don't worry 'bout what you don't know
> Life's a Dance you learn as you go

For the past 20 years, I'd been too busy to live life … or to even have a life! And as I listened to these words, I realized that I needed to let go of working so hard and dance my way out of the corner I'd been in.

In fact, I believe I was born to dance. And I was born a blonde. A blue-eyed blonde who was the apple of her daddy's eye. Shortly before I turned three, my mom packed her friend's car with some essential belongings and left town with my older brother and me ... while my dad was at work. He had no idea what was coming. None of us did.

We were always safe, and Mom took very good care of us. But for many years, I experienced a haunting loneliness that I couldn't explain ... until I reconnected with my earthly dad. But I don't want to get ahead of my own story here. Only to say that I learned that my mom had been abused as a child, and as a result, she was very confused about men. She adored my three uncles, but didn't trust any other men.

So she poured herself into being a mom and helping others. A very creative woman, she spent her days cooking and baking and sewing beautiful dresses for me with all kinds of ribbons and bows. I loved to dress up ... but oh! how much I hated those home permanents!

Being from a divorced family was much more unique in the 1950s than it is now, and apparently something for a child to be ashamed of. I didn't realize this until my Bluebird Troop visited the radio station when I was 7 years old. The announcer began a live interview with each of the girls. I was so energetic – all twirls and smiles – and so excited to get to be on the radio. When the man came to me, he asked the same questions he had asked of the others, but there seemed to be something very wrong with my answers ...

> "What's your name?"
> "Debby"
> "What does your daddy do?"
> "Oh, I don't have a daddy."

The expression on the nice announcer's face changed drastically, and he quickly removed the microphone from in front of me and started talking to the next Bluebird. I was immediately flooded with an overwhelming sense of shame.

It was clear to me that I'd said something terribly wrong, but no one told me what it was. And I was too afraid to ask.

I've never forgotten that day, nor the sadness of my dad's absence. Despite my inner turmoil, however, I busied myself with school, where I was a great success. And had my mom not transferred a lot of her fearfulness to me, I'm sure I'd have been enthusiastically climbing trees, playing baseball, and getting muddy with the best of them. Mostly because I loved to hang out with the boys. My brother hated it. What an annoying little sister I must have been!

But boys were so very interesting to me, and there weren't many girls my age to hang out with ... that is, until I was in the third grade, and my best friend Deanie and I became inseparable. She lived across the street, and one of our favorite activities was to choreograph dance routines to show tunes and perform them in the empty apartment above her parents' house. What fun!

However, we were never allowed to dance with boys. Well, almost never. Deanie's mom and dad were opposed to dancing with boys on religious grounds (or any other grounds, for that matter), but my mom didn't see a problem with it. So one weekend, Deanie spent the night at my house, and my mom drove us all the way downtown to a teen dance. Of course, Deanie's mom just happened to call while we were gone, so Deanie ... and my mom ... got into big trouble! Needless to say, my mom wasn't very happy with me either for putting her in such an awkward spot with another parent.

It was our one and only dance ... until our Junior-Senior Prom. For some reason, Deanie's parents allowed her go to that one. And we both had dates, so they knew we'd be dancing with boys. Go figure.

Church was always a big part of our family life, even when my parents were together. Sunday mornings, Sunday evenings, Wednesday night prayer meetings. I remember asking Jesus into my heart during Vacation Bible School one summer, and true to His Word, He came in to stay.

But other than going to church, Mom didn't contribute much to our spiritual understanding or growth. I don't remember ever hearing her pray, though she did read her Bible a lot. In fact, she kept it near her rocking chair and underlined her favorite verses with a pen. Sadly, that was her only testimony.

Like most adolescents, I had a hard time during junior high. Thankfully, our ultra conservative Midwestern church provided the Rules for Living, and we had the world's absolute best youth group. We went roller skating, camping, boating, and for hayrides. But we never engaged in my favorite sport: dancing.

Trying to make sense of it all as an adult, I composed a brief bio that I shared with folks who asked about my religious upbringing. It went something like this:

> My dad was Pentecostal, and my mom was Baptist. Their marriage didn't last. Go figure.
>
> We moved into a house between the First Baptist Church and the Nazarene Church, and my mom chose the Nazarenes. So I was raised a Nazarene by a Baptist mom. Go figure.
>
> I married a Lutheran when I was 18 years old, and we became United Methodists. Our marriage didn't last either, yet the Lord has remained faithful. Go figure.

I've often told people that I know firsthand what it's like to be in a painful relationship. We were so young ... too young. Neither of us had the support we needed. And we never learned to dance with one another.

Then suddenly I had primary custody of our three sons. So I really needed to figure out guys ... for their sake.

And after our divorce, I did finally learn how to dance with boys. It was great exercise and something that made me smile during a very stressful time of my life. But the joy faded, and I soon realized I needed to focus on my future.

Encouraged by the women at my church, I enrolled in college. I had supported my husband through his studies, but missed my turn at school. And because I was now a single mom, I thought I had no choice but to give up that dream. However, My Heavenly Father had a better idea. And He reconnected me with my earthly dad, too!

What an amazing surprise that was! Although we'd not seen each other for several decades, we were like Two Peas in a Pod. Similar in personality and sense of humor ... and my boys said we even looked alike! My sweet dad, however, was quick to say, "But she's prettier than me!" Oh, how that still makes me smile! Thanks, Dad!

Once in college, I thought I'd given up dancing ... again. So you can just imagine what a kick it was for me to be given the opportunity one semester to teach an aerobic dance class at College Church three nights a week. Here I was dancing in the church! What an amazing, imaginative God we serve!

Four and a half years and a Whole Series of Miracles later, I graduated *magna cum laude* from MidAmerica Nazarene University. My family and friends put me on a plane headed for graduate school in California.

Once again, I thought, "Alas, no more dancing for me!"

I eagerly busied myself with studies at Rosemead School of Psychology at Biola University, loving every minute of it. I'd always been very fond of school, so it was only natural that I'd keep going once I had the chance. I loved school so much, in fact, that for 8 years following graduation, I was part of the Undergraduate Psychology Faculty at Azusa Pacific University. During 6 of those 8 years, I also taught at Biola University. What a blast that was!

What? No dancing? Well, yet another surprise opportunity arose for me as a graduate student during one of my practicum assignments. Working at a day rehabilitation center for persons with severe and chronic mental illnesses, I was expected to lead two groups. My chosen topics were "Spiritual Concerns" and "Country Line Dancing!" Both groups were quite popular, and our rooms were quickly filled to overflowing with exuberant participants.

Thank you, Lord!

Then another break from dancing occurred as I completed my pre-doctoral internship at the University of Kansas in Counseling and Psychological Services. I did some teaching there as well, plus taught a class at my *alma mater* that spring. How cool to get to hang out with all my undergrad profs! Like they say, it was déjà vu all over again.

But I could hardly wait to get back to Southern California. I had the privilege to teach at Azusa Pacific University at the same time I was completing my licensure requirements under Dr. Jennifer Fee at Vision Quest Psychological Services. Great opportunities, but alas, no dancing.

I must pause here and tell you about my experience with career counseling. You'll see the humor – and the Lord's hand – in it, I'm sure. Several years before I began my studies, I visited our local community college to enlist their expert assistance with deciding on what I wanted to be "when I grew up." The results of my aptitude, achievement, and interest assessments suggested that I might like a career as (a) clergy, (b) psychologist, or (c) professional dancer!

Funny, eh?

Oh, did I mention that I've always been a Romantic?

At this point, anyone who gets within three feet of me knows that I'm hopelessly romantic. My online presence confirms it, as does my personal video collection, which is comprised of 99% romance.

In fact, I get razzed a lot for my tendency to quote lines from romantic movies ...

*As Good As It Gets. Christmas in Connecticut. Cinderella.
The Cutting Edge. Dan in Real Life. Double Wedding. Emma.
Enchanted. Ever After. The Ghost and Mrs. Muir.
He Married His Wife. Hope Floats. Joe vs. the Volcano. The Kid.
Mad About Men. The Mask of Zorro. Miss Congeniality.
Once Upon a Mattress. Overboard. Pretty Woman.
Pride and Prejudice. The Princess Bride. The Runaway Bride.
The Shop Around the Corner. Sabrina. Sense and Sensibility.
Shall We Dance? Sleepless in Seattle. Something's Gotta Give.
Tangled. What Women Want. When Harry Met Sally.
Yeomen of the Guard. You've Got Mail.*

We all love the "meet cute" at the beginning of a movie. It reminds us of the excitement, hope, and joy that we experience at the beginning of a relationship.

Next, the boy wins the girl ... or at least gets her attention. Then he screws something up ... or at least she thinks he did. And the rest is about getting her back. All of which takes less than two hours, of course. We're set up from the start to believe they'll get together and live happily ever after. It's the way love's meant to be, right?

So I wondered, "Why do our own love stories often end so painfully?" Well, because love takes more than two hours to develop. And because – despite popular belief – it isn't always the guy who screws things up.

That's why I love my job. I get to help couples figure out what has gone wrong with their relationship. But most of all, I love to help the boy win back the girl. Yes, I'm hopelessly romantic. ... Or am I a Hopeful Romantic? Yes, that's it. I'm a Hopeful Romantic.

But it isn't just about the movies ...

As a Licensed Psychologist, I've studied the Psychology of Men and Traditional Masculinity at the graduate and post-doctoral levels. I even taught a class at Azusa Pacific on this very popular subject. What I've learned is that most women don't have a clue about men's experience, and that most men don't know how to explain it.

So I put together a series of classes for women who want better relationships with the men in their lives. And the men I've seen in couples counseling have said they would like me to teach them about women, but they've also admitted they would probably never attend a workshop about understanding women.

The Best Things Happen While You Dance!

Couple dance is a beautiful example of what makes a romantic relationship work. The man takes the lead, and the woman follows. He guides and protects her. She influences him, even as she admires him … and makes him look good to anyone who's watching. As Danny Kaye sang in *White Christmas*, "Even guys with two left feet come out alright … if the girl is sweet."

So for several years I'd wanted to find a way to use dance as a part of my experiential approach to helping couples grow closer to one another. But I was limited in my capacity to teach dance … especially to the men.

*Then a **Miracle** Occurred …*

The very day after I presented my very first women's seminar, "The Princess and the Frog" at Newsong Church in Irvine, California, I met the totally amazing Fred Judkins, a completely delightful Christian man who shares my beliefs about the God-given differences between men and women … and how we should treat one another.

That sunny Sunday afternoon, I had the opportunity to dance with this very gracious and funny guy, and was not only fascinated by his dancing skills, but also by his gentleman's demeanor. It wasn't long before I was totally mesmerized by the way he talked about a man's role in the lives of women.

Needless to say, I soon realized that what he had to say fit perfectly as the counterpart to what I was teaching women and how I was helping couples. It wasn't long before the wheels started to turn and I prayed, "Wow, Lord. Here is someone who can teach the men to dance!"

Several months later, Fred graciously volunteered to help with our First Annual Victorian Valentines Dance, which evolved into this book and our *Dance With Me* workshops. He is a very gifted man who loves the Lord, and I know without a doubt that folks will enjoy knowing him – almost as much as I do.

My life's a dance that's still in the process of being choreographed by My Loving Heavenly Father. I've known some sadness and some pain, and I'm sure I will experience it all again, at least if I remain this side of Glory for very long. But I also get to experience unspeakable joy!

M. Scott Peck simply noted, "Life is difficult." And I'm convinced that it's even more difficult to go it alone. That's why God sets the lonely in families (Psalm 68:6), and why He ordained marriage (Genesis 2:18).

In Part 1, *Dance With Me*, we'll take a look at the music, as well as the basic steps of the couple's dance. In Part 2, *Just Follow My Lead*, we'll be talking about what a woman needs from her man that will invest her with an irresistible desire to follow him. Part 3, *Do You Love Me?*, will be much longer because men are complicated, and women have very strong beliefs about them – false beliefs that are frequently perpetuated by men themselves. Finally, in Part 4, *The Sweethearts Ball*, we'll describe the beauty and the challenges of a romantic dance between a man and a woman.

It's a lifelong learning process. I don't pretend to have all the answers ... I'm still learning to dance myself. But I do know a few steps, and I'd like to share them with you. Some steps are intuitive. I hope other steps will cause you to reconsider what you think you already know. As Will Rogers said, "It ain't what we don't know that hurts us. It's what we do know that ain't so."

So whether you are already coupled and seeking to improve your dance, or single like me and hopeful about finding the perfect dance partner, please know that my fervent prayer is that your life, as well those who know you, will be richly blessed by *Dance With Me*.

Warmly,
Dr. Debi Smith
Newport Beach, California

Part 1
Dance With Me

AN INVITATION

Love

Who's not a hopeless romantic
deep down in their secret soul?
Even the most jaded
falls under its beguiling control.

A star filled night and a golden moon
hypnotize and tease
casting lovers under the spell
of kisses from a summer breeze.

The promise of the unknown
beckons even the most shy
do you dare step forward in faith
or let love's whisper pass you by.

For a simple dance all by yourself
can certainly be done
but the dance of love is far more complex
because two must dance as one.

~ *Marilyn Sweet*

Dance With Me

Dance with me, I want to be your partner
Can't you see, the music is just starting
Night is falling, and I am calling
Dance with me

Fantasy could never be so thrilling
I feel free, I hope that you are willing
Pick the beat up, and kick your feet up
Dance with me

Let it lift you off the ground
Starry eyes, and love is all around
I can take you where you want to go

Dance with me, I want to be your partner
Can't you see, the music is just starting
Night is falling, and I am calling
Dance with me

~ Orleans

I've been dancing single for a very long time, so it seems odd – even to me – that as a female psychologist, I would choose a professional specialty in men and romantic relationships. Most psychologists focus on the individual, whereas marriage and family therapists focus on ... well, marriage and family.

However, I've never been able to resist the beauty of intimate relationships ... mostly because I love to dance. And I love men. And I love romance. And I love God. But not necessarily in that order, of course.

If you think about it, the phrase *dance with me* is actually an invitation – a sweet request – to join together in the creation of something beautiful as a couple. These words are neither to be uttered in a demanding tone, nor with expectations that you merely do as I say. Both the request and its response are intended to be something we do together in harmony with one another and with God's plan. The dance applies to married people for sure, but also to those of us who are hopeful about finding romance. We enter into the dance desiring to learn from each other the essential steps we need to know in order to be able to dance as one.

As we do so, we learn more about ourselves, other people, and Our Heavenly Father. It's wonderful. It's difficult. And it's always worth it ... even if our toes get stepped on.

The term *dance* is not new in the field of psychology. Many counselors have referred to the emotional patterns of our interpersonal relationships as a dance. The term has been used to describe one or more negative cycles of interactions – something people need to change. However, we will be taking a very different approach: that a couple dance is something that can be done well. For that to happen, we must be attuned to God's Word and to one another.

In fact, a couple dance – such as a waltz – is the perfect example of what makes a romantic relationship work. The man takes the lead, and the woman follows. He guides and protects her. She influences him, even as she admires him ... and makes him look good to anyone who is watching.

But many of us enter marriage never having learned to dance well as a couple. We often fail to even recognize what type music is playing! The perfect music is heavenly, of course. Ephesians 5 provides the melody, and our partner's needs, desires, and responses help us know which steps are in tune ... and which ones we need to adjust. The success of our couple dance depends on our willingness to learn from one another with tenderness, sincere interest, love, and respect for who God created us to become as members of the Body of Christ.

We'll start at the beginning with Chapter 1, of course, which is all about the heavenly melody, the *Romance of Ephesians 5*. Chapter 2, *Attached and Attuned*, will explore some of the findings of scientific research on intimate relationships and what is required in order to create an enjoyable dance for both people involved. Are you ready to get started?

Then queue the music ...

 *Chapter 1*

THE ROMANCE OF EPHESIANS 5

Dance. What a perfect metaphor! And what a great way to experience the romance of Ephesians 5! Indeed, there's nothing more beautiful than watching a couple swirl around the dance floor in perfect harmony … unless it would be the beauty of being the girl who is being swirled! If you've not yet had that pleasure, just trust me when I say that it is totally divine … and a very romantic experience that lies ahead for you … whether or not you actually ever set foot on a dance floor!

Using some of the most romantic words in the Bible, the Apostle Paul describes what the couple dance (male-female relationship) should look and feel like for a pair who have chosen to follow Christ's example as Head, with the Church as His Bride. In short, these simple truths tell us how to engage and interact with one another in order to be successful in life and in marriage.

> *Submit yourselves to one another out of reverence for Christ.*
>
> *Wives, submit yourselves to your own husbands as you do to the Lord. For the husband is the head of the wife as Christ is the head of the church, his body, of which he is the Savior. Now as the church submits to Christ, so also wives should submit to their husbands in everything.*

Husbands, love your wives, just as Christ loved the church and gave himself up for her to make her holy, cleansing her by the washing with water through the word, and to present her to himself as a radiant church, without stain or wrinkle or any other blemish, but holy and blameless. In this same way, husbands ought to love their wives as their own bodies. He who loves his wife loves himself. After all, no one ever hated their own body, but they feed and care for their body, just as Christ does the church – for we are members of his body.

"For this reason a man will leave his father and mother and be united to his wife, and the two will become one flesh." This is a profound mystery – but I am talking about Christ and the church. However, each one of you also must love his wife as he loves himself, and the wife must respect her husband. ~ Ephesians 5:21-33

First, Paul instructs us to submit to one another as members of the body of believers in fellowship with one another, which naturally will apply to husbands and wives as well. However, just *how* husbands and wives are to submit to one another is easily – and very frequently – misunderstood in our current culture. Some Christians ignore the concept of submission altogether, whereas others read Paul's words as permission for husbands to dominate and/or abuse their wives. Neither option creates a loving, romantic relationship. And we need to work to get it right from the start – before we're even dating.

Basically, Paul tells us that men and women are equal, yet different. Both are created in the Image of God to work together in harmony, and each is designed for a unique role in the relationship. One is designed to lead, and his partner's *trust* and *respect* are essential for him to be able to lead well. The other is designed to follow, and her partner's *love* and *understanding* are essential if she is to follow well.

That's what *Dance With Me* is all about – helping couples and singles learn exactly what loving submission looks like in the 21st Century. It doesn't involve acting out extremes on either side, but is a balance of working together as God intends – of learning to dance well. Dancing requires that we know our respective roles from God's point of view, as well as our own needs and limitations – and our partner's needs and limitations.

No doubt, every Christian woman loves the idea of being swept off her feet by a godly man who knows how to lead – gently and confidently, protecting her and guiding her through life. What Christian woman would not want a husband who is willing to die for her, as Christ died for the Church? A woman has no problem submitting to a man she truly believes has her best interest at the forefront of everything he does. However, many women – even those who are already married to a Christian man – feel like they can only long for this experience, having no idea how they can help translate this dream into their reality.

And a Christian man loves the thought of having a godly woman to lead – a woman who is confident and provides him with gentle feedback about how well he's doing ... especially if she's adept at making him look good in the process. What Christian man would not want a wife whose desire is only to please him and be his partner? The fact is, most men are inwardly unsure of themselves and rarely get the positive feedback they crave – though they rarely, if ever, ask for it.

First of all, learning to dance well means learning your partner. Gals, what does he need, what does he enjoy, what pleases him? Guys, what does she need, what makes her smile? Learning someone takes time. Lots of time. I've always advised men and women only to marry someone they'd be willing to spend the rest of their lives getting to know ... because it will take that long ... an endless and a welcome task ... made equally complicated and pleasurable due to our God-given differences. Oh, joyous rapture!

Men and women are not only different by nature, but are also unaware of just how *different* they are ... and *how* they are different. Most people believe – and this is one place where men and women *erroneously* agree – that women are more sensitive than men. In reality, research has shown that men are actually more sensitive than women! However, men are sensitive about different things than women are, and they express their emotions differently. We can't understand that until we examine our responses and interpret them according to the correct template. But more about that later ...

We also speak different languages. That is, the same words don't hold the same meaning for men as they do for women. So many couples who are experiencing relationship problems seem to need an interpreter. In fact, what I mostly do during a couple's counseling session is translate "what he just said" into words that she can understand, and then translate "what she just said" into words that he can understand.

So on the surface, it seems like poor communication is the problem. But like so many other things in life, there's more to it than that. The lack of connection and understanding run deeper than mere word-choice. There are some fundamental biological and social differences that lead to very different world views – a situation that's not easily resolved ... especially when it prevents us from even *trying* to understand.

At the root, we find the commonly held belief that "men are simple," and "women are complicated." I hear that a lot ... so much so that it seems to be universally accepted as an immutable fact of life – one that gets in the way of any hope for a better connection ... or dancing well together. Author Grantley Morris puts it this way:

> There seems a common belief that women are more complicated than men. This belief has perhaps contributed to more marriage problems than any other belief. Men generally conclude from it that women are so hard to understand that there's no point in even trying to understand them. (Women who try to maintain an aura of mystery may be doing so to their own hurt.) And women tend to assume that men are so easy to understand that there is no need to even try to understand them better.

So when it comes to better understanding the opposite sex,
it's often the case that men feel defeated before they start
and women barely see a need to start.

And, as human beings, we all tend to interpret one another through the lens of our own life experience. Having very different life experiences means that learning your partner will mean learning a new language – at least well enough to communicate the basics. We can let the music do the rest.

We also have different ways of looking at life, and we have different needs and different wants …

In studying the psychology of men and intimate relationships, I've learned that men need bullet points and bottom lines. Therefore, *Just Follow My Lead* – the man's section of this book – will be very brief, which actually works out well because women are really simple. As it turns out, we only want a few things from you. However, many of us believe you "should already know," and that tends to make things seem much more complicated than they actually are. All you'll really need is your very own *Magic Decoder Ring* to interpret what she wants and/or needs. I promise to give you one.

Do You Love Me? – the woman's section – will be much longer because men are more complicated than women are, and women like lots of details, which naturally requires lots of words and lots of examples and lots of details … and where to write to ask your questions when there hasn't been enough explanation … or enough detail.

There's no doubt that your man is unique … and so is your relationship. I get that! Even so, I'll try to give you some basic principles about men. It'll be up to you to ask your fella if they apply to him. He will be flattered that you care enough to ask … and he will tell you. Just be sure to pay close attention! Remember, your goal is to learn *your* man.

Before I launch into those sections, however, I would like to share what we have learned from research about the nature of intimate relationships. It turns out that we all need the same things in order to develop healthy relationships, but as we will discover in Part 2, our nature (capacities we were born with as male or female humans) and our nurture (how we were parented as boys or girls) have both played important roles in who we turn out to be by the time we begin to be interested in the opposite sex. Stay tuned …

ATTACHED AND ATTUNED

*For this reason a man will leave his father and mother
and be united to his wife, and the two will become one flesh.*
~ Ephesians 5:31a

Parents are important. Without them we wouldn't exist. And without them, we wouldn't know how to be in relationship with one another. Therein lies the source of some of the problems we encounter in romance. Dad and Mom taught us more than we realize … and some of it's not so good … as if we were not sinful enough on our own to cause relationship troubles. But do not despair! What has been learned can be unlearned. Nothing is written in stone.

The Scientific Theory of Emotional Attachment

The beauty of science lies in its confirmation of God's amazing creativity. We can see what works and what doesn't. And we can cooperate with God's desire for redemption of everything under the sun. Science cannot save us from our sin. Only God can do that for us by grace through faith in Jesus Christ. But we can learn, like King Solomon, by observation and analyses. And that's where today's science fits with God's Kingdom.

Although a number of researchers (see the Bibliography at the end of this book for a detailed list) have studied the process of human development from a psychological perspective, those who have contributed to the Theory of Attachment have provided us with some easily understood information about who we are, particularly in relationship to one another – and even to our Creator.

Dr. John Bowlby, a British psychiatrist, was among the early researchers in Attachment Theory, and he explored the impact of the mother-child relationship. He noticed that, in addition to their need to be fed and protected, children also have a need for very strong *emotional* bonds with their parents or caregivers. He proposed that we come into this world with an *attachment system* that assures our survival and safety in relationship to significant caregivers. When a baby is distressed, this attachment system motivates him or her to seek closeness to a safe person.

If someone is consistently *available* and *responsive* to the baby's needs, then negative emotions (e.g., anger, fear, sadness, hurt) are reduced. The child feels soothed and begins to develop the capacity to self-soothe by recalling the feelings associated with being comforted by a loving caregiver. Based on these memories, a child develops a "template" for relationships that includes the beliefs that are essential for secure emotional attachment: (a) I am lovable, and (b) I can depend on others to be loving toward me and to help meet my needs.

Secure Emotional Attachment

Subsequently, other researchers tested Dr. Bowlby's ideas and found that interactions between a child's temperament and the caregivers' responsiveness result in more or less secure styles of attachment. As stated in the previous paragraph, our early experiences provide us with both images and emotions that form the template that serves as a pattern for understanding how to form relationships and how dependable we can expect them to be. We learn about ourselves in relation to others based on (a) their availability and responsiveness to us, as well as (b) how well we do in getting others to respond to our needs.

Although later experience may change our beliefs about the security of our relationships, we most often seek out people who fit the template we already have. So, generally speaking, if we developed an insecure style of attachment during childhood, it will continue to haunt us throughout adulthood ... unless a later relationship (e.g., with a human being or even with God) provides a series of new experiences that help us become more emotionally secure.

Research continues in the field of Adult Attachment Theory, with new information and more intricately defined models being formulated in recent years. However, I prefer to use one of the original models in explaining attachment because of its simplicity and elegance in explaining the way a couple can create a beautiful dance, as well as in describing the various ways that things can sometimes go painfully wrong.

You can assess your own emotional attachment security in a variety of ways, but one of the easiest is to take a look at what happens when you feel stressed out. How you handle stress (and express yourself) involves both your feelings and your actions. We all get a bit anxious when we're under stress ... some more so than others, of course. Whenever you experience anxiety (worry, concern, fear, frustration, feeling trapped or stuck), then your ability to communicate is also affected.

You've also learned what actions to take when you're stressed. Do you seek other people out to help you with your stress? Or do you pull away from others and handle stress on your own?

Securely attached men and women still experience anxiety, but at lower levels. When they're worried or concerned about something – inside or outside of the relationship – they seek out their partners to help them talk things through. After their talk, they feel less worried. If that sounds like you, you are probably more emotionally secure.

A securely attached man feels confident taking the lead in the Dance of Romance. That's not to say that he never has doubts or anxieties. However, when he does, he talks to his partner about it. He's learned that it's okay to be vulnerable with her – that she is a safe person for him. He knows that she will be available and responsive to his needs.

She never shames him or makes him feel bad about himself, but instead knows how to comfort him without making him feel like a little boy in the process. This can get a little tricky for women who don't really understand the differences between men and women in this regard. (Please read Part 3: *Do You Love Me?*)

A securely attached woman feels safe following her partner in the Dance of Romance. She trusts him and is confident that he has her best interest in mind ... that he won't drag her around the dance floor like a rag doll ... or leave her standing there alone. She also trusts that he's paying close attention to God's guidance, as well as to her needs and her desires. She knows he's open to her input and her feedback. It's not that he always does whatever she says; it's just that he is always willing to listen to her ideas.

She respects his developing leadership abilities, asks him for what she needs when she feels anxious, and can rest secure in his arms as he choreographs their Dance together.

Insecure Emotional Attachment

The model we'll use defines three insecure attachments: Preoccupied, Fearful Avoidant, and Dismissing. Each has its own distinctive set of problems in learning to Dance.

Preoccupied Attachment is characterized by a negative view of oneself (I'm *not* okay) and a positive view of the other person (you *are* okay). These individuals feel highly anxious in their relationships, demonstrate a high level of dependence on others, and invest a significant amount of energy in relationships that may not necessarily be in their best interest to maintain. The Preoccupied man or woman will have difficulty loving, trusting, and respecting a partner in the Dance, and may appear controlling or dominating. The greater his or her anxiety becomes, the more likely he or she will appear to be angry, demanding, and critical.

Fearful Avoidant Attachment is characterized by negative views of both self and others (*neither* of us is okay). These men and women are socially/relationally avoidant because they are fearful of their own vulnerability in intimacy. They anticipate that others will be hurtful and believe that they don't deserve to be treated well due to perceived personal shortcomings. Although they may secretly desire it, they are not likely to get on the Dance floor – both literally and metaphorically – because they fear looking bad, feeling rejected, or being criticized.

Although *Dismissing Attachment* is also characterized by social/relational avoidance, the interpersonal dynamics are quite different from those of a Fearful Avoidant attachment. Men and women with a Dismissing attachment style have a more-or-less positive view of self (I *am* okay) and a negative view of others (You're *not* okay). They place little, if any, value in intimacy and are consequently counter-dependent in their relationships. That is, they often choose independence and autonomy over relational interdependence. In other words, they don't care much for Dancing. At best, they think it would be too much bother ... and at the worst, it's just plain silly.

There you have it. Many of us can identify a multitude of ways to make our relationships *not* work. As promised, however, we're going to maintain our focus on what *does* work. What works is being *available* and *responsive* to our partners "in the here and now," and caring about how our personal actions might affect others – especially the person we love most in this world.

For the most part, I think I'm getting pretty good at being *available* and *responsive* to my dance partner. And although I've become known as an "expert" on the psychology of men and relationships, the Lord teaches me more about both topics every day.

Once during a dance lesson, Fred and I were demonstrating the "swing" step, and he was telling the men how to make it enjoyable for the woman. He said, "Guys, you just pay attention to how your sweetie's body is responding to the music and to you, and then you match her."

Huh? For years I'd been telling women that they need to follow their guy – to match him. So I was more than a little taken aback by his verbal instructions.

I looked up at him and spontaneously proclaimed, "You're matching *me*? I thought I was matching *you!*"

He just smiled at me and gently replied, "We're matching each other."

Now I ask you, "How sweet is that?" A perfect way to play out Ephesians 5:21 – right in the middle of a dance lesson!

As couples, we must learn to pay attention to one another's needs and to be responsive to one another in light of the unique design and purpose given to us by Our Creator. Remember it was Christ who announced the revolutionary idea that husbands and wives are equal before Heaven, at the same time recognizing specific roles for each. So if we want to dance well together, we will need a more complete understanding of our biological differences, as well as the differences in how we were nurtured. So that's where we are heading now ...

Part 2
Just Follow My Lead

EVERYTHING A MAN NEEDS
TO KNOW ABOUT WOMEN

Dancing Cheek to Cheek

Heaven, I'm in Heaven
And my heart beats so that I can hardly speak
And I seem to find the happiness I seek
When we're out together dancing cheek to cheek

Heaven, I'm in Heaven
And the cares that hang around me through the week
Seem to vanish like a gambler's lucky streak
When we're out together dancing cheek to cheek

Oh! I love to climb a mountain and to reach the highest peak
But it doesn't thrill me half as much as dancing cheek to cheek
Oh! I love to go out fishing in a river or a creek
But I don't enjoy it half as much as dancing cheek to cheek

Dance with me
I want my arm about you
The charm about you
Will carry me through to

Heaven, I'm in Heaven
And my heart beats so that I can hardly speak
And I seem to find the happiness I seek
When we're out together dancing cheek to cheek

~ Irving Berlin

Guys, wouldn't it be great if you could exceed the wisdom of Dr. Sigmund Freud? Despite all his work with women in exploring the possibilities of "a talking cure," rumor has it that he died still wondering what women want.

Actually, we're not that complicated, but poor Siggy didn't have anyone to translate for him. Now you're going to get the inside scoop! In the next few pages, I'll share with you what a woman wants and needs from a man that will invest her with an absolutely *irresistible* desire to follow him.

Now how cool is that? Way cool.

Most of us believe that women are more complicated than men, and that's simply not true. In fact, most problems men have with women can be solved using a minimum of words and energy.

Really? What a relief!

You see, the problem is *how you see the problem*. And the problem you think you see is probably not the problem at all. Women have just been taught to communicate in a very different way than you were. Our sex is actually *required* to communicate in a *Secret Code (e.g., going around in circles, using too many words, never getting to the point).

In the next few pages, I'll break the code for you so you can figure out what she needs and wants.

Because this section is written for men, it'll be brief. You guys like to get to the point. I love that about you.

---

* A Word of Encouragement: I'll be spending a lot of time helping women learn to be more straightforward in their communication with men. We'll all be a lot happier for it.

Chapter 3

WOMEN ARE SIMPLE

Women are different by nature. We can't help it. We were born that way. And truth be told, you guys like us this way. In fact, there's no one you would rather dance with than a girl, right?

However, the very things that draw you to us are the very things that you find confusing. You've probably wondered with Professor Henry Higgins in *My Fair Lady*, "Why can't a woman be more like a man?"

But that's not really what you want. You love the fact that she's emotionally sensitive and not as big or as strong as you are. But you're also very confused that so much depends on how she *feels*. And she feels *a lot*.

And she can talk forever and ever and never get to the point. She looks to you to solve problems for her ... sometimes. But just as often, she gets angry if you try to solve a problem for her ... especially if her feelings are involved. Sheesh.

What you probably don't realize is just how differently she's been treated her entire life ... just because she's female.

From the moment her expectant parents found out she was a girl, she has been viewed as sweet and delicate.

For example, as a toddler, she got picked on by another child at the park, and her mom or dad moved in quickly to intervene. She was given lots of comfort, understanding, hugs and kisses, and reassurance that she was cared for. Her tears meant something – helping her communicate that something was wrong. She felt like she mattered. Childhood was a very different experience for her than it was for you.

She was probably trained to be a pleaser. At the very least, she learned that nice girls never come right out and ask for what they want, that they take turns, and that they must always consider how other people might be feeling. So she learned to use a very tentative language, which now to you seems vague at best and just plain crazy-making at its worst.

She knew another girl was her best friend because they shared secrets with one another. Unlike your childhood friendships that focused on shared activities among a whole gang of guys, two-by-two proved to be the best pattern for her. Add a third girl to the equation, and it was an emotional disaster waiting to happen. Sounds weird, huh?

As if the tearfulness and the vagueness and the secret-sharing aren't enough, the differences between male and female communication are extensive. You wouldn't think the same English words could hold such different meanings for two people brought up in the same culture, but they do.

For example, take Sean and Nicole. They decided to take a day trip from Newport Beach to Solvang one Saturday. They'd been on the road for a couple of hours when Nicole said, "Do you want to stop and get something to eat?"

"No," Sean replied and kept driving.

Nicole's feelings were immediately hurt. But why? She asked if he wanted to stop, and he merely answered her question. What's the problem with that?

The problem was that he hadn't answered the question she was really asking. If he knew the Secret Code, he would have known that what she said was her tentative (feminine) way of saying that she was hungry and asking him if he would stop for her. He would have known to counter with, "Sure. We can if you'd like. Are you hungry?"

Another of the reasons women are so tentative is that we are often labeled as "needy" ... a most uncomplimentary descriptor.

And yet another reason is that we want to please *you* first and foremost, which is the honest explanation for our seemingly wishy-washy reply to your question, "Where do you want to go for dinner?"

When we say, "I don't care. Wherever you want to go is fine," we are just trying not to sound demanding ... and trying to please you ... which actually has the opposite effect. And yes, I am going to tell the women to stop doing that to you.

Sigh.

In sum, she's different from you in that ...

- so much depends on how she feels,
- she values conversation for conversation's sake,
- and much of her self-esteem depends on what she thinks you think of her.

Yes, your opinion actually matters more than anything. She was raised to be a pleaser, and you are the one person she wants to please the most.

And if you are like most men, you would like to make her happy ... if you only knew how. But she unknowingly sets you up to fail by not being specific enough. We're going to work on that one for you, too. I promise.

But first, let's talk about what she needs from you. And in order to do that we'll have to break the Secret Code …

Chapter 4

DECODING A WOMAN

I know you won't believe this, but you men are actually far more complicated than we are. Otherwise, the chapters about you would the short ones, and the chapters about us would be the long ones. Honestly, pretty much everything she struggles with in your relationship – as even she would confess – fits into one of the following three categories:

1. I don't feel like I'm special to you.
2. I don't feel like I'm attractive to you.
3. You hurt my feelings.

As promised, this will be a short chapter, filled with bullet points and what-to-do's. You'll get enough detail to get the idea. And if it's not enough, please let me know. I'll be happy to elaborate online at www.OCChristianCouples.com

Bullet Point #1: Make her feel special.

So much of her self-esteem depends on what she thinks you think of her. Not what you *actually* think of her, but what she *thinks* you think of her.

Now you're probably thinking, "Great. How in the world am I supposed to be able to manage *that* one?"

The good news is that it's actually much simpler than you realize, and it's something that you already have a natural desire to do: Be her Hero.

Men love to be Heroes, so it comes naturally to you to behave like a Knight in Shining Armor to every woman you meet – to the lady at the market who can't reach the last can of Who Hash on the top shelf, to the poor gal with the flat tire who can't figure out how to work the air machine at the gas station, and even to your grandmother.

But as a romantic partner, you may have forgotten the importance of being Gallant – Chivalrous, Courteous, Polite, Gentlemanly, Thoughtful, Gracious, Suave – towards her, especially if it seems like she doesn't *appreciate you. (*I promise to work with her on this one for you, too.)

So if you want her to follow your lead, the first thing you'll need to do will be to put forth extra effort in helping her realize that you are, first and foremost, *Her* Knight – and that *she* is the One Lady that you cherish above all others.

I can't emphasize this enough ...

This part is absolutely *crucial* if she already is – or if you want her to become – your wife and lover!

If you haven't been Gallant for a while, there's no way you can go into this expecting an immediate payoff. Winning her trust will take some time – that is, you will need to convince her that you're treating her well just because you love her, and that you are not trying to get something in return ... like sex. Whatever you do, remember that it is simply your *Gift* to her, then be sure to act accordingly.

Where to begin ...

Every girl knows that a Hero does simple, everyday things to make you feel special. He opens the door for you and allows you enter a room first. He pulls out a chair for you at the table. When you go to a restaurant – even if it is only your local Subway Sandwich Shop – he asks what you would like, then places your order for you saying, "The lady will have ..." adding his own order last. Very sweet and very, *very* irresistible.

He makes eye contact when you are talking, which clearly communicates that all he cares about at this moment is you. He looks into your eyes and derives great pleasure in just seeing you looking back at him. He gives you a hug ... not because he wants sex, but because he finds you so adorable. And if he wants to take it over the top, he'll ask you to dance with him!

A guy can't help but be a Hero to his Sweetie as he glides her around our Dance floor. It's essential that couples keep the fun in their friendship, and Vintage Dance is the perfect place! Great melodies and easy to learn Dance steps. And you don't have to spend a fortune to enjoy an evening of Style and Elegance when Two Hearts are beating – and Dancing together – in three-quarter time!

Dance With Me

Relationship Workshops

Men enjoy a hearty breakfast as Dr. Debi explains everything they need to know about women ... in 90 minutes or less!

Ladies relax over a lovely luncheon, then enjoy the afternoon as Dr. Debi unravels the Mystery of Men.

Couples end the day with a laughter-filled evening that provides an unparalleled opportunity to practice what they've learned in our charming 19th Century Ballroom!

Victorian Dance is stylish, elegant, simple-to-learn, ... and very, very Romantic!

There are lots of ways to keep your relationship alive and well with fun and friendship, so be creative. But honestly, guys, Dancing is the absolute best, even if you feel like you have two left feet. She'll love your efforts, so why not give it a try?

Magic Decoder Ring: Seven Top Clues that tell you she needs to know – by your *actions* – that she's special to you:

1. She says she wished you still _____
   (*talked to one another, held hands, had fun together*).
2. She complains that you never take her out anymore.
3. She stops getting gussied up (dressed up or fancy).
4. You know you treat her differently than you used to.
5. You spend more time ____ing than you do with her.
6. You haven't taken her anywhere that would give her an excuse to get gussied up in more than six months.
7. You haven't felt like a Knight in Shining Armor since … well, you just can't remember when.

Be on the lookout for more clues that she's missing her own Knight in Shining Armor. And if you're not sure, start being Gallant anyway. Who says you need a clue to do that?

Bullet Point #2: Tell her she's pretty.

This point's the simplest one. Women spend a lot of time, energy, and money trying to look as just pretty as they can. And as she gets older, she'll start doubting that she could still be attractive to the opposite sex.

If she's already yours – or if you want her to be yours – you won't want some other guy beating your time! Tell her yourself that she's pretty and/or cute … *on a daily basis!*

Of course, you must be absolutely, positively sincere about whatever you say. Flattery is cheap and meaningless, and she'll see right through it. Don't go there. Trust me. It's simply not worth the price.

Magic Decoder Ring: Seven Top Clues that tell you she's unsure she's still attractive to you:

1. You never ask her to Dance.
2. You don't tell her she's pretty or cute.

3. You don't look into her eyes when she's talking.
4. You don't look at her longingly as you once did.
5. She says, "Notice anything new?" and you don't.
6. She complains that you're looking at other women.
7. You haven't asked her out on a date since ... well, you just can't remember when.

Be on the lookout for more clues that she's questioning her attractiveness. Then pay her a sincere compliment each and every day. But who says you need a clue to do that?

Bullet Point #3: Just say you are sorry.

A woman's feelings can get hurt very easily, especially by the man she loves. Her feelings are important, and she needs you to appreciate that about her. In fact, feelings are *primary* for most women. When our feelings get hurt, we go into defensive mode. And everyone knows the best defense is a good offense.

So we often look and sound angry when, in fact, our feelings have been hurt. At that point, we'll either withdraw or attack, depending on our emotional attachment (Review Chapter 2). Hurting her feelings is tantamount to Crushing Her Spirit. Nothing good can happen until Her Spirit has been revived. When you learn how to help her with that, you'll reap rewards beyond Your Wildest Dreams. And it only takes three steps:

1. Notice that you hurt her feelings. That means you have to be paying attention, right?
2. Then say, "I'm sorry" or "I'm sorry I hurt your feelings." (Note: Say nothing more. Say nothing less.)
3. If she's angry and/or yelling at you, you'll need to say it at a distance. If she is crying, move in close and hold her hand or put your arm around her. Or if you're not physically present, you can tell her you wish you were there to hold her hand or to put your arm around her. That works almost as well because this is one of those cases where it's mostly the thought that counts.

This concept is so simple, yet often so very difficult for you guys to grasp. So much so that I frequently spend an entire couple's counseling session explaining it to a man who objects to the apology on the grounds that he's done nothing wrong. The story goes something like this ...

She fixes his favorite dinner as a special surprise for him one evening. He gets tied up at work and doesn't to call to say he'll be later than usual. When he arrives home, he doesn't notice anything special. He hurts her feelings.

She's noticeably upset and may even use words to tell him so, which may sound to him like attacking, criticizing, or blaming. He tries to explain what happened, thinking this will make her less upset. She hears his words as defensiveness ... that he's making excuses ... and trying to minimize the impact of his actions upon her feelings.

It's really simple, guys. Her feelings were hurt ... by you. She understands that sometimes you get tied up at your job, and she knows that it can be hard for you to call when you're dealing with a crisis at work. That's *not* what she needs you to apologize for. Not even close!

She *only* needs you to apologize for *hurting her feelings*.

Here are three bullet points for clarification:

- You are *only* apologizing <u>for hurting her feelings</u>, which you *did* do ... whether you meant to or not.
- She's the only one who knows when she's hurt. So *never* say, "I'm sorry *if* I hurt your feelings." It's tantamount to telling her she is crazy. And despite what you might think, she's *not* crazy: She's a girl!
- You are *not* apologizing for staying late at work.

When I explain this to a man during a counseling session, he invariably looks at his partner and says, "Really? *That's* all you want? That would *work*?"

She says, "Yes, that's all I want."

And then he doesn't believe either one of us ... until he gives it a try. For once, she's actually telling him specifically what she needs from him in a given moment. If he's wise, he'll listen and give it his honest effort.

To ensure you don't miss this very important part of the equation, as you are telling her you are sorry, remember:

Anger = Away (as in "keep your distance")
Tears = Touch (as in "get close enough to comfort her")

A Final Word About Women: Anxiety

The vast majority of women deal with anxiety on a daily basis. We're anxious about a lot of things, especially when it comes to men. Here are a few examples that apply to most women:

Her physical safety. Ask her, "When was the last time you were afraid for your physical safety?" You'll probably be surprised by her answer. More than likely, it was sometime within the last twenty-four hours.

Women constantly scan the environment for danger, especially if they have to be out after dark without you for protection. We look for danger so automatically that we can't imagine that you men don't do the same. We don't realize that you're confident you can protect yourself if you need to do so. However, we must plan our defense, which usually involves (a) escape and (b) calling for help.

Displeasing you. Women are taught from early childhood to be pleasers ... something that intensifies with the onset of that wonderful phenomenon known as *puberty* ... mostly because we have been led to believe that there is a verifiable shortage of desirable men. Historically, that has been true. And it feels even more true to a woman who is unsure of herself to begin with.

We fear that if we displease you, you might reject us or abandon us. Sometimes, a woman might appear to be overly confident. In this case, what actually may be her Fear in Disguise can come across to you as "she doesn't really care about me."

When in doubt, assume that she fears displeasing you.

Feeling unimportant. For the last several years running, the most popular post on our *Psychology of Men* blog has been "Why Do Men Stonewall?" Stonewalling is withdrawing or refusing to respond to your partner. For you, it may be a response to your own confusion or feeling overwhelmed when she's upset. Or you may just try to stay calm in the hope that she will also calm down.

However, when you stay calm, it feels like you're just being nonresponsive to her, which only serves to make her even more anxious. The message your nonverbal behavior sends is that you simply don't care that she's upset. In reality, it's counter-productive, and actually will increase her anxiety and frustration, propelling you both into the same negative cycle that you are trying so hard to avoid.

It goes something like this, doesn't it? She begins a conversation with something that sounds harsh – something that feels like it came out of the blue. She's actually tapping on the door, trying to make contact with you.

When you fail to respond, she assumes you didn't hear her, so she talks a little louder. Now she's knocking on the door wondering if you are even in there.

Your heart races as you think, "Here we go again. This is not going to be good." You try even harder to remain calm, hoping that she'll settle down.

You might even try talking firmly or "logically" to try to calm her … which only feels condescending to her. Shaming is not exactly sending her the message that she can depend on you to be there for her when she needs you.

If she wasn't really angry before this, she is now. Her feelings are seriously hurt, and she's in defensive mode (please refer to Bullet Point #3). She's now coming through the door with a two-ton wrecking ball, and she's determined that you *will* hear her out.

To you, she's in some sort of crazy rage, and you may begin to wonder if she has serious mental health issues. So you'll have a difficult time realizing that, underneath her anger, is a huge backlog of fear. She may have a difficult time recalling her original feelings, too. But your best bet is that she started the whole conversation at least a little worried that her concerns would be totally unimportant to you – based on verifiable evidence from any previous stonewalling you have done.

I have to tell you that I really do understand why you guys do this so often and so automatically. It makes total sense to me, and I do my best to educate the gals about how their emotions impact you. However, you must understand what happens for her as well. Basically, when a woman is emotionally flooded, and her partner shuts down during a disagreement, she's most likely to say she feels:

abandoned	isolated	shut out
blown off	lonely	undesirable
dismissed	pushed away	unloved
frustrated	rejected	unwanted

Well, *that* was not what you were going for, right? You only wanted her to be reasonable – to stop making such a big issue out of whatever it was – or at least not to attack, blame, or criticize you in the process.

There *is* hope for redirecting this scenario, and the best place to start is with Bullet Point #3. If it happens a lot, you may want to find a good couple's counselor – one who gets where *you* are coming from, as well as *her* position.

Without a doubt, this isn't a comprehensive explanation of all women … or even of *your* woman. But if you apply these

Basic Principles in your relationship, you *will* see a change. Remember, she may not trust you at first. In fact, you can count on a least some skepticism. If things have been rocky for a while, she may wonder what's happening at best and may suspect you're trying to manipulate her or that you're "up to no good" at the worst.

Just remember that a woman often worries about her physical safety, as well as whether or not she is displeasing and/or unimportant to the man she loves. But that's not all. We have other fears, too.

A major one that often remains unspoken for many a Christian woman is that her man will not be the Spiritual Leader of their family. So she takes over, and she doesn't do it well. Although it's better for the man to take the lead, especially with the children, she reasons that a *female* Spiritual Leader is better than *no* Spiritual Leader. However, once she's taken on that role – before or after marriage – it'll be very difficult for you to step up to the plate. So *please* be the leader, in every sense of the word.

> *The most important task you have been assigned is to continually direct and redirect your loved ones toward Christ. Only He can meet all their needs ... and yours!*

Leadership is your responsibility. You were designed to take the lead. God created you with all that it takes right there inside of you. It's a learning process, for sure, and no man comes into this life knowing how to lead. So get all the support you can.

As a husband, you'll be held responsible before God for your family. God knew it was Eve who took the first bite of the apple, but He came looking for Adam. You can believe me when I say I know that women can be difficult to love sometimes. I'm one of them, remember?

But please don't give up. Lean on the Lord, and allow Him to guide you. Watch the movie *Fireproof*, and get your hands on a copy of *The Love Dare* book, find a good Christian couple's counselor. Do all you can, especially if you have children still at home.

Even so, I know that there are some situations where nothing a man can do will save his marriage. It takes two to create a couple dance, and if the unbeliever leaves, you are not bound in such circumstances (1 Corinthians 7:15).

And you won't be alone. Unfortunately, divorce is every bit as commonplace among Christians as it is among non-Christians. Find a good church, a group of Christian men, and/or a Christian therapist to help you navigate the rough waters ahead, again – especially if you have children. You'll want to remain active in their lives and be the kind of dad they need. They're about to enter rough waters, too.

Well, I did *not* intend to end up on *that* note. I'll have to think of something sweet to end this chapter with ... and not a preposition! [*Oops. Did I say that out loud?*]

So how's this for a goal? Imagine having this Cole Porter song play through your subconscious all day, every day ...

When shades enfold
The sunset's gold
And stars are bright
above again
I smile, Sweetheart
For then I know I can start
To live again, to love again
When day is done
And night comes on
Until the dawn
What do I do
I clasp your hand
And wander through
slumber land
Dream dancing with you

We dance between
A sky serene
And fields of green
Sparkling with dew
It's joy sublime
Whenever I spend my time
Dream dancing with you
Dream dancing
Oh, what a lucky windfall
Touching you, clutching
you
All the night through
So say you love me, dear
And let me make my career
Dream dancing
To paradise prancing
Dream dancing with you

Part 3
Do You Love Me?

THE PSYCHOLOGY OF MEN
AND RELATIONSHIPS

As promised, Part 3 is much, much longer than Part 2. The reason is that men are complicated, and women have very strong beliefs about them – mostly false beliefs that are frequently perpetuated by men themselves.

Another equally important reason this section is longer is that I believe when men get the essentials they need from us to be successful Dance Leaders, they naturally respond to us just the way we need – and want – them to respond. I've watched it happen over and over again in my office.

My underlying assumption is that women don't understand how a man thinks, what he feels, and why he behaves the way he does. Simply put, men are complicated because there's no explanation for them … at least not that he offers.

So women are confused about men. And men are confused about themselves … sometimes. But mostly, they operate by Very Different Rules than women do. And one of those Rules says that there's no need wasting time and energy on explaining the obvious. However, what seems obvious to a man is utterly confusing to a woman. The goal of *Do You Love Me?* is to end – or at least begin to end – the confusion.

You may be quite surprised to learn that nature and nurture play out in male development in ways that simply don't go that way for us. These are Really *Big* Differences that make his behavior confusing … and him very desirable! In other words, he has very good reasons for being the way he is. And once you understand his "template," you'll have the capacity for a greater appreciation for who he is as a man.

In addition, we'll be exploring the "Stages of a Man's Life," which are very different than they are for a woman. His age and where he is in the process of life will provide even more explanation and understanding of why he does things the way he does. I promise, he *will* make sense to you … at last!

Beyond that, you'll also want to know what he needs from you … mostly because he never asks for what he needs. And there's a good reason for that, too!

And of course, you'll want to know how to change him!

Change him? ... Wait just a minute! ... What did you just say? ... Is that even possible?

Stay tuned ...

Chapter 5

MEN ARE COMPLICATED

A few years ago, a young couple came into my office for their first session of marriage counseling, and right away I could tell that the husband didn't want to be there. He took one look at me, and by the expression on his face, I could just imagine what he was thinking.

"Great. Just great. Our last therapist was a man, and he seemed pretty good, but my wife didn't think he was helpful. So now we're going to talk to a *female* counselor? Oh, brother! Here we go again. Only this time, I'm going to get it in stereo. Ok, suck it up, buddy, and get ready to go three rounds with not one, but *two* women hammering away at you for the next 45 minutes. And at the end of it, you get to write the woman a check. I'm such a lucky guy."

His wife appeared a little anxious – and a lot frustrated. She began with a very intense explanation, even before they were seated. "He never talks to me. In fact, all I get is the cold shoulder. Whenever I try to discuss an issue, he tunes me out! He just sits there, staring at the TV. Sometimes he gets up and storms out of the room ... without saying a word! He's just so insensitive. I don't see how this marriage will ever work if he's not willing to talk about things. I'm ready to give up. I've tried everything I can think of to get him involved with the family. How can he *not care* about his own wife and family?"

I listened patiently to her lament, and out of the corner of my eye, I could see her husband slowly sinking into his end of the sofa.

I nodded understandingly at his wife, then said, "I can see how hard you're working at this – trying to make your marriage work – and how distressed you are. This is really, really hard for you."

Anticipating my alliance, she sat up straighter and listened intently as I joined her in her frustration. "Being in a painful relationship is incredibly difficult, I know. And you know what else? ... We've actually been lied to."

The husband continued to sink a bit deeper, while a slight smile stole across his wife's face as she waited for more confirmation of what she thought she already knew – that she was right, and he was wrong.

"Yes," I continued. "We've been lied to. We've been led to believe that men are insensitive jerks. That they're not in touch with their emotions – if they even have any. That they just don't get it. It's like the elevator doesn't stop on that floor. But the truth is ... men are actually *more* sensitive than women."

The wife tipped her head sideways, like a bright-eyed cocker spaniel who couldn't believe her ears. I imagined she thought, "What? This can't be right! This woman is *not* going to be helpful. She obviously doesn't know *anything* about men!"

Anticipating her confusion, I supported my statement with some research findings, and she appeared to be a little bit more interested. I imagined she was thinking, "Well, maybe she does know a *little* something about men. Maybe she *can* fix my husband ... or at least get him to talk to me!"

At the other end of the sofa, her husband seemed to breathe a sigh of relief, sat up a little straighter, and almost smiled. If he had been more verbally inclined at that point, he might have said something like, "Hey, this woman gets us guys. This therapy stuff might actually work this time. Thank you, Lord! ... I just hope my wife pays real close attention."

Men Do Think About Their Relationships – A Lot!

As we will discover, most men process their thoughts internally – before they speak. They are taught to do so. Because they often don't share their thoughts with their partners, women erroneously assume men don't think about the future ... or devise a plan for getting their families from Point A to Point B. Nothing could be further from the truth!

According to author Gordon MacDonald, men have a lot of serious thoughts – about a lot of stuff.

> *Among all these thoughts are the private thoughts. They are the ones I hold on to most tightly for fear that, if exposed, they might show a side of me that almost no one knows or would understand: the side that includes thoughts of possibilities, failures, dreams, fears, desires, shame, beliefs, regrets, memories – both good and bad – and, well, the list goes on and on.* (p. xviii)

The Making of a Man: Nature and Nurture

Researchers and philosophers originally debated about the role of nature *versus* nurture in directing the process of human development. Findings have been inconsistent in terms of which is more powerful, our biology or our environment. Consequently, they sort of gave it up and focused their studies on understanding the interactions between these primary two factors.

Because psychological experiments on human beings (as well as many animal experiments) are unethical, we are left to our observations of what exists naturally within the world – not unlike King Solomon. Without the benefit

– or the risk – of studying cause-and-effect relationships, we can only recognize correlations among various factors and suggest probabilities.

The bottom line, then, is that we can only report what's likely to happen and conclude that we can't really know anything for sure. That is, in applying any research finding to real-life situations, we must admit that it all depends upon a multitude of factors. However, what we learn can be helpful in providing some probable – or at least plausible – explanations for why people are the way they are.

The same is true for the information shared here. Although something *probably* applies to most men, it may or may not apply to *your* man. Therefore, you are encouraged to summarize what you glean from this book and to ask your guy whether or not it fits him. At the very least, he will be flattered that you cared enough to ask. At the very best, you will have had an opportunity to learn more about him, and that is always a very, very good thing.

Nature: Men are more sensitive than women.

Researchers have found evidence that male infants are more emotional than female infants from birth until at least six to twelve months of age. Infant boys cry more frequently and intensely, coo and smile more often, and experience more rapid fluctuations in emotional states than do girls. However, by two years of age, there is already a noticeable reversal in verbal expression; and by six years of age, there is a noticeable difference in facial expression as well.

Furthermore, boys seem to have a natural tendency to express their feelings more through *action* than by talking about them. Whatever the reason, boys demonstrate an ability to avoid overt responses to emotion between four and six years of age – interestingly, about the time they usually enter kindergarten. (We'll explore some possible explanations for that in a moment.)

So fast forward to adulthood. Once they grow up, do men even *have* feelings anymore? Or have they simply been disconnected from their own emotions? Marital research conducted over the past several decades suggests that men really do have feelings – very strong ones – and that they are highly aware of each and every one of them.

In one particular study, couples volunteered to be observed interacting with one another. Video cameras recorded their spontaneous interactions, and researchers coded their behavior for analysis. Over time, the researchers began to notice that some participants tended to be very emotionally expressive (i.e., visibly and audibly upset or angry) during a disagreement, whereas their partners were not.

So the researchers devised a method to help determine what might be going on that wasn't directly observable. They asked the couples to sit in facing chairs and instructed them to discuss something about which they disagreed. Each person was connected to equipment that registered respiration and heart rate, as well as how much each wiggled in the chair. The data they collected showed that, although the seemingly non-responsive partners appeared to be totally cool and calm, their heart rates frequently rose above 95 beats per minute when things got tense.

Interesting, eh? It appears that cool and calm on the outside does not equal cool and calm on the inside.

I've found in counseling a wide range of couples, it's often the men who are most successful at *appearing* to maintain their composure. They may not be emotionally expressive, but their bodies sure are!

So it's no wonder that men often fail to respond verbally. They're probably too busy regulating their pounding hearts. After all, we know that one of the Rules of Manhood is "Never let 'em see you sweat." And if men take action when they feel emotions ... well a pounding heart *is* part of the *fight*-or-*flight* response. Which of those responses do you prefer when it comes to you?

So what about nurture?

Going back to Attachment Theory (Chapter 2), you'll recall that healthy human development relies heavily upon the processes of relationship, especially upon our primary need for emotional connection with someone who is *available* and *responsive* to our needs. However, boys typically experience relational trauma that girls rarely do. It usually goes something like this ...

As a toddler, he got picked on by another kid at the park, and his mom or dad held back to see what he would do. When he came to report the offense, he was required to provide explanation. His tears were something shameful. Big boys don't cry, so stop whining and figure out what to do. He learned that he was on his own – that he would have to solve his own problems somehow. Childhood was a very different experience for him than it was for you.

He knew he had friends because of their shared activities. Unlike you and your best friend in childhood who shared intimate secrets, he was busy hanging out with a whole gang of guys who did stuff together. No secret-sharing.

And according to research psychologist Dr. William Pollack, every boy learns "The Boy Code" as a matter of course:

- *Be a Sturdy Oak*
  Whimpering, crying, complaining, or any sign of weakness is strictly forbidden.
- *Give 'Em Hell*
  Risk-taking behavior of a macho, invincible, sometimes violent, high-energy superman is encouraged.
- *Be the Big Wheel*
  Dominate others and refuse to let anyone know you actually feel like a failure or like life is out of control.
- *No Sissy Stuff Allowed*
  This last commandment is what Dr. Pollack believes prohibits boys from expressing any feelings or urges

that might be viewed as feminine, such as dependence, warmth, empathy. Great, huh?

Where's mom?

Mom is usually our first relationship, and until a boy reaches about three years of age, his relationship with his mother is very similar to that of a girl with her mother. Then, sons and mothers begin to relate to each other in a different way than do daughters and mothers, and the vulnerable feelings that arise around this disconnection may have very profound implications for the rest of male relational development.

American culture in general supports this disconnection, which researchers refer to as *normative developmental trauma,* which a girl isn't required to experience. A boy is pressured to disconnect from his mother – usually through shaming by other boys and men. In addition, his mom is expected to support his turning away from her, even if she feels it is wrong to do so. He must be declared different from her, compares himself to others, tries to be unique, and feels bad when he is unsuccessful.

Perhaps as a consequence of her own misunderstanding of men, a boy's mom is usually the one to fit him with his first "gender straitjacket" through emotional shaping that begins at birth and continues throughout the life span. In the process of attachment and (frequently traumatic) separation, she actively (though often unwittingly) participates in the hardening process that shames boys into suppressing their empathic and vulnerable sides. One of the first things a mother wants to know is whether the child is a boy or a girl. As soon as she knows, the process begins.

Dr. Stephen Bergman also noted, "Often the boy is taught not to listen to his mother trying to maintain connection, or to listen with a certain suspicion, and if he does listen, not to respond to her." As a result, he may become paralyzed both emotionally and relationally by his own ambivalence – his intense longing for close emotional connection and the fear of his vulnerability at the same time. Very confusing and sad … and very, very lonely.

At this point, he needs to identify with someone – ideally, with a caring, available father. However, his father may also be encouraging the mother-son disconnection, be recovering from his own relational trauma, and be unable to provide him with the empathic relationship he so desperately needs.

Consequently, the boy moves from a mother connection to a father *dis*connection. Rather than learning to maintain the emotional ties essential for development, he learns to disconnect from the process of relationship, and may never learn how to be emotionally close with another person.

Male Relational Dread

Thus, not having learned to deal with unpleasant emotions in relationship when he was a boy, a man may continue to feel intensely afraid of conflict, as well as connection. Bergman labeled this emotional experience using a highly descriptive term: *male relational dread*. A man's fear is characterized by a sense of inevitable, never-ending disaster and an expectation of immense and irreparable damage. And often the closer a man feels to a woman, the more intense his dread. He feels unsafe, guilty, incompetent, and ashamed in this uncharted territory.

Under the pressure of needing to fix things, he is overcome by an ever-increasing sense of dread. Although a man may want connection desperately, he may withdraw, strike out, tune out, change the subject, joke, make nice, or simply fall silent in an effort to deal with his anxiety.

Gordon MacDonald put it this way:

> *Among the first private thoughts in the male are ones that center on the issue of* feelings, *which most of us are taught, should rarely, if ever, be acknowledged. The don't-cry-act-like-a-man message comes early in life. And a boy*

learns to master his tear ducts and force his face into an expression that would make a stoic proud. The feeling may be unbearable, *he thinks,* but there's no way I'm doing to let you know it. *From that point forward in the male life feelings and emotions are increasingly stuffed somewhere. Fear, sadness, anxiety, smugness, anger, joy, loneliness, disappointment:* don't let them be seen, deep-six them, make them disappear, so far away, so deep, so buried that no one, even I, will ever know they were around. (p. xix)

It's indeed most unfortunate that many men have sufficient evidence from their own relationships with women that disconnection may actually be the better, safer way to go. Men – no doubt with good reason – do not trust women to let go of their false images of men, and to accept and appreciate their vulnerability as human beings.

However ... the good news is that you have the power to change that experience for *your* man – starting today! Simply be a *safe person* for him. And if you don't know what that looks like, find a knowledgeable counselor who can help you develop the understanding and skill required. You will both be the better for it.

Created With a Purpose

Man was created first. Then woman was created for man. No, that's not a popular idea, but it's right there in the *Bible.*

> *For man did not come from woman, but woman from man; neither was man created for woman, but woman for man.*
> ~ 1 Corinthians 11:8-9

If we back up to the very beginning, we see that men have needed us from the start. Man was originally created with a need for relationship – and God's answer was a woman.

> *The Lord God said, "It is not good for the man to be alone. I will make a helper suitable for him."*
> ~ Genesis 2:18

I like the way Pastor Mike Erre said it when he spoke at Mariners Church in Irvine, California:

> [Genesis 1] *God created mankind in His Own Image. In the Image of God he created them. Male and female he created them .... And instead of it being good, it's very good .... The Bible begins with the fundamental absolute and unambiguous declaration of the equality between men women .... Both male and female are needed to reflect fully the image of God.*

> [Genesis 2] *Adam, flying solo through the animal kingdom ... God looks at him ... the Lord God said "It is not good for the man to be alone. I will make a helper suitable for him." Now in English, that sounds like, "Adam, you're very important, so you need an executive assistant" ... or "You need someone to kind of clean up your mess." But the word helper ... in Hebrew ... it's a very strong word. It's actually used of God. God as a rescuer. So David will cry out to God, "O, God, You're my help. You're my strength." That's the same word, so you can translate this, "God looked at the man and saw that he needed a rescuer and provided woman."*

Wow. That is *powerful*. What an important role we have to play! However, Pastor Mike went on to say that – as part of the curse noted in Genesis 3 – the woman's desire is to control, manage, and fix her husband. And that man will toil his life away. And they won't get along with one another. That doesn't sound so good now, does it?

However, we can now give thanks to the Lord for the hope we have through our faith in Jesus Christ, who sets things right again. In Ephesians 5, we learn that man is to *love* his wife and be willing to die for her ... as Christ died for the Church. So far, that sounds like the Best Good Deal for Womankind. But that's not all there is to it. There's that part about the wife's submission, remember?

Clearly, we are created as partners. Essential partners in the work of the Kingdom of God. Through Christ, we are redeemed to fulfill the purpose for which we were created.

Man is the Leader, and woman is the Follower. He's not a dictator, and she's not a silent, meaningless subject. More about that later ...

Fortunately, when we get things back in their proper, Heavenly perspective, man has what he needs to do his job, to live out his life doing what God designed him to do. And man was created to be especially adept at four things (five, if you count parallel parking): protecting, providing, problem-solving, and pleasing. Yes, they all begin with the letter "p." That makes it easier to remember. How cool is that?

My Protector

Man protects instinctively. He protects the people he loves ... and sometimes even people he doesn't love ... and sometimes even people he loves – or doesn't love – who happen to be angry at him at the time.

Remember that he's more sensitive than a woman. Here's where this characteristic comes beautifully into play. His radar is alert for danger, and instead of analyzing his emotions, he takes action ... or gives you advice or tries to solve the problem. Which you often hate because you don't understand his intent. You erroneously believe he's trying to fix you just to shut you up. Although that may be partially true (sorry for being so frank), it's mostly that a man doesn't like to see someone he loves suffering. He wants the pain to stop ... and to stop *now*. So he gives you advice. He's trying to protect you from further hurt. You can appreciate how really sweet that is of him ... when you understand why he's doing it.

However, his sensitivity can backfire in a heartbeat. If he feels like he is being attacked, blamed, or criticized, he will go on the defensive ... to protect *himself* rather than you.

And here is the really sad part: Most of the time, you have absolutely no clue that you might be saying or doing anything that could be even remotely related to attack, blame, or criticism. This is where we need to understand the power of our language, and that words often hold very different meanings for a man than they do for a woman.

For example, I was counseling an engaged couple who had hit a roadblock on their way to the altar (metaphorically, not literally). As they struggled to understand one another, the woman looked at her fiancé and said, "I hate that I'm causing you so many problems. Maybe you'd be better off without me. Maybe it'd be better if I just walked away."

You can understand that statement, right? She sounds like she's willing to sacrifice her happiness for his. Wrong.

That's not what he heard at all! What he actually heard was, "You'd better get your act together, Bud, or I'm outta here."

He was deeply wounded by her statement and didn't want it to show. So he stiffened his upper lip, and shut her out ... to protect himself.

When I told her how he heard her statement, she looked as us both in disbelief. He confirmed my translation from *female expressive language* into *male receptive language*. What she'd said was not what he had heard.

His sensitivity to rejection ... to not being good enough ... to his failure to please her ... had colored the meaning of the words he heard. He was listening though the filter of his emotions ... through his intense fear of being found inadequate.

The fear of being inadequate is certainly not unique to this one particular man. All men are unsure of themselves. And every man fears being emasculated.

And women have no less than a bazillion ways of telling men they don't measure up ... of taking away the power they have as men.

Here are just a few ways you might be communicating to him that you believe he is inadequate ...

- You smirk or roll your eyes at him.
- You give him advice by saying something like:
    - Have you ever thought about ...?
    - Why don't you ...?
    - You should ....
- You talk about him to other people like he's not there.
- You laugh at him ... when he's not trying to be funny.
- You blame him for whatever has just gone wrong, usually trying to make yourself look better.
- You correct or criticize him. This one is powerfully emasculating when you do it in front of other people.

A few months ago, I was waltzing with a friend at a very festive ball, when the couple ahead of us tripped, and the woman crashed onto the floor. Her partner, who was obviously concerned, responded immediately to help her to her feet. Her response? She glared at him, shaming him by her facial expression as well as her words. I'm still not sure for whom I felt more empathy: her for falling ... or him for being yelled at in front of a ballroom full of his peers.

Note on Repairing a Disconnection: If he shuts you out when you're talking, stop and ask him what he heard you say. If he's honest with you, he'll tell you that it felt like an attack, blame, or criticism. And if he tells you that, believe him. It does *not* mean that's what you were *trying* to do. It just means that what you said got lost in translation, and you can try again ... but use different words.

My Provider

Men love to provide for us. They see themselves primarily as Providers. In fact, there was a time when the primary determinant of a man's self-worth was how well he was able to provide for his family. Maybe this is still that time. You may have noticed that one of the first things a man tells someone is what he does for a living. His job, career, or profession is a major part of his identity. As old-fashioned as it sounds, most men still don't like being taken care of financially by a woman. It's not "a pride thing." It's just who they are … it's in their DNA.

As a 21st-Century woman, you probably believe that you can make it on your own. Unlike our sisters before us (e.g., Elinor Dashwood in Jane Austen's *Sense and Sensibility*), most of us have ample opportunity for employment that fits our skills and training. There are other reasons we struggle financially, but the oppression we face in society is most certainly not what it used to be.

In fact, our social standing changed significantly in wartime … specifically during World War II. Our men were shipped overseas to fight, and we were left at home to run the country. When the guys returned home, we seemed to be saying to them, "What do we need *you* for?"

In this country, women have been running the show for a long time now. However, we also need to talk about the huge price we pay in doing so. Life isn't like it was in Jane Austen's day. Women have gained a tremendous amount of freedom, and rightly so. But have we gone too far in our quest for equality?

It's not just that we miss being protected, guided, and held by our man. It's also that, when women wear the pants, we lose something essential of who we are created to be … at all levels, intellectual, emotional, relational, physical, etc. In a word, we force ourselves to operate in "survival mode" and may never have the opportunity to thrive!

God designed women to be adaptable, which is a good thing. We have what it takes to rally when needed, but we can only do it for the short term. As a way of life, it can destroy us.

A female speaker (a layperson, not a psychologist) recently reported that men are better equipped to lead because of their naturally higher testosterone levels. Something like 30 times as much? So – according to her – when women need to "step it up," they must rely on adrenaline, which is only a short-term solution – for any human being. If we rely on it long term, we destroy our bodies. Makes sense to me.

But that's not to say men don't run on adrenaline far too often as well, but that it's not their first resource in the drive to survive. If not psychosocially/emotionally emasculated – which may actually reduce testosterone levels in males – men have what it takes to go farther and faster than a woman does before their bodies begin to overuse their sympathetic nervous system for day-to-day survival.

In addition, there's actually a body of research that provides evidence that, in order for women to survive in business, they must have the ability take on masculine qualities ... especially when it comes to communication. In other words, they have to learn to walk and to talk and to act like a man, or they will fail in a Man's World.

That isn't to say that women can't be good providers. Many of us have had to be the sole providers for our families. But women need to stay connected with and value their feminine qualities, and not try to become men. The converse is also true. Men need to be tender and sensitive and caring, but with the unique style that men have. We should not try to make our men into women.

My Problem-Solver

Men are wonderful Problem-solvers. Whenever you have a problem, he loves to be able to solve it for you. It brings him great satisfaction. It enhances his masculine sense of self. He loves it ... if you take his advice, that is. But that's not always what we're looking for, is it?

Sometimes we just want him to listen and provide empathy. We can probably solve the problem by ourselves. If he jumps in and starts to tell us what we should do, we get angry ... usually because he hasn't heard the whole story. And let's face it: We easily turn a simple story into a long and drawn out affair. It's just what we do.

For example, my friend was telling her husband about when she went to the mall to pick up some makeup she'd ordered from Macy's ... you know the kind that makes your skin feel like silk? It's the greatest creation ever! And as she was on her way to Macy's she walked past Pottery Barn, which was on the left side of the very busy courtyard, which at that very moment was filled to the brim with the most adorable gaggle of giggling children, playing on the indoor playground equipment with their mothers chatting cheerily nearby. The kids were so cute, and one little girl had on the most darling outfit. It had a great big strawberry applique on the front and the cutest little ruffles across her bottom. And her blonde curls bounced as she toddled around the courtyard with her friends. The scene reminded my friend of when her own kids had been toddlers, and about how much she misses them now that they've gone away to college. She paused just a moment watching the children and sighed, then immediately spied something in the window of Pottery Barn that drew her attention away from the playgroup. She'd been thinking about redecorating her bedroom, and there it was ... right there in the window of Pottery Barn ... the most beautiful Arista Palampore duvet cover and sham in a most charming delicate blue. Well, we all know that the most sought-after fabrics of 18th-Century France were those printed with indigo, a natural dye imported from the Far East and the New World. It was immediately apparent that this bedding would fully capture the exotic, romantic feel of those antique French textiles she'd been wanting – complete with a lush garden printed in soft color on an ivory ground. It would be perfect, especially since it was on sale, she reasoned. So she entered the store and struck up a conversation with another woman who was looking at the same display. They shared their decorating ideas, as well as the fact that their husbands saw no need for the change. And before they knew it, they realized they both went to the same college ... though several years apart. They ended up going for coffee, and next week they're all (yes, husbands included!) going to meet at the club for dinner. Isn't that amazing?

Sigh.

My friend obviously – and obliviously – doesn't know this simple fact: that men listen in sentences (looking for a problem to solve or a purpose for relating the information), where as women talk in paragraphs (sometimes volumes). My friend's poor husband was frustrated, and so was she.

As women, this kind of conversation is natural to us. That's how we connect with one another. Remember, when we were kids we knew someone was our best friend because we shared our secrets with one another. We do it with all our women friends, and they don't get annoyed. They counter with more stories, and we enjoy getting to know one another in that way.

But he's not a woman. And he's never going to be a woman. We're thankful for that, yes? Most men don't derive pleasure from feminine banter. It can wear them out … quicker than we realize. Men use fewer words, but more about that later …

Bottom line: There is a simpler way. Before you start talking, give him the bottom line. Is there a problem you need his help with? Or is the current problem that you just need someone to tell a story to? If you let him know that you just want to share something with him – pleasant or unpleasant – just because he's your Best Friend … that you just want him to listen and be interested in you … that you don't want him to fix any particular problem … that you'll only talk for five minutes, he'll most likely be happy to do that for you. But only for five minutes – really.

Why do men get worn out by our long stories? Because they're working so hard to try to find the bottom line. And they look for the bottom line at the end of each sentence. But then we start a new sentence, and he still has the previous sentence in his head, and the new sentence doesn't seem to follow the previous sentence … and he glazes over. Poor guy.

Just remember that his problem-solving is another way he shows you that he cares for you. He doesn't want to see you anxious or hurting or distressed or angry ... especially angry at him. Which leads us to his next purpose ...

My Pleaser

This is one that so many women don't completely grasp. Most men I meet – even the ones who are coming to counseling to work through some very difficult relationship issues – simply want their wives to be happy. Their bottom line is that they desperately want to please their wives, but they just can't seem to figure out how to do it. Sadly, most men would be willing to settle for an end to the arguing.

Men hate conflict. Many shut down in an attempt to slow it down ...or to avoid it altogether. We call that *stonewalling*, and it invariably has exactly the opposite effect than the one he's hoping to achieve.

As a couples therapist, I've had ample opportunities to observe how hard women work at their relationships. Whenever something's wrong, it's usually the woman who notices it and wants to talk about it – to figure out where the disconnect lies and to fix the problem. Here's an example of a frequent complaint from our online Relationship Survey:

> *We have problems agreeing on the way in which we will deal with problems. I want to deal with them when they come up, and he wants to think about it on his own for a long time and hope the problem goes away before we talk about it.*

Chances are, this woman won't be able to wait for him to bring up the problem again. She'll be miserable waiting for him to say something. At best, she'll feel like it's just not that important to him. At worst, she'll feel like *she's* just not that important to him. As the hours and days tick by, she'll start to feel more and more anxious about their relationship.

Definition: Stonewalling is withdrawing or refusing to respond to your partner. For men, it may be a response to their own confusion or due to them feeling overwhelmed.

In addition, most men learned early in life that they must come up with the answers to their problems on their own, so this behavior also makes sense in this regard.

But for women, stonewalling by a partner creates excessive anxiety – and anger. The surprising side of stonewalling: It's actually much more damaging to the relationship if it's the *woman* who does the stonewalling! It seems that men have a much tougher time when we shut them out than we do when they shut us out. It's in the research. Go figure.

So men often give in to their wives just to bring an end to the argument. When he gives in to you, he gives up the Power he needs in order to be your Protector, Provider, and Problem-solver just for the sake of ending the argument. It's emasculating.

And how disagreements are resolved has a significant impact on the level of satisfaction for both partners in a marriage, as measured by a variety of relationship assessments, such as the *Locke-Wallace Marital Adjustment Inventory*. The scoring for this questionnaire weighs each answer differently (higher is better) in response to the following statement:

> *When disagreements arise, they usually result in:*
> *(a) the husband giving in (0 points)*
> *(b) the wife giving in (2 points)*
> *(c) agreement by mutual give-and-take (10 points)*

Perhaps this is where men's greater emotional sensitivity comes into play? Or are we back to the fact that they need us ... and they need us a lot? Grantley Morris reported:

> *In a survey, marrieds were asked to name their best friend. Women typically named another woman, whereas most men either named their wives or confessed to there being no one in their entire world that they could call their best friend. This highlights how isolated most men are, and how dependent they are upon their wives for companionship. There simply seems to be something about being male that causes this aloneness. It is so basic that it*

is even found in the animal kingdom. In a wide range of animal species, females generally group together with each other and with the young, whereas mature males are loners, usually relating to their own species only to fight other males or mate with females.

It might take a husband years to realize just how mistaken was his presumption – and his wife's presumption – that his wife understood him. The typical husband's reliance upon his wife for companionship and emotional support makes it a chilling experience when he finally concedes she seems incapable of understanding him. Can you imagine how devastating it is to feel there is no one on the planet who knows and understands you to the degree that you crave and deserve?

If genuine, and not a mere pick-up line, "My wife doesn't understand me," are among the loneliest words in the English language. Not only that, the inability of most men to get close to each other usually leaves him feeling unable to turn to anyone for solace, unless it be another woman. He is strongly pressured either to try that, or try to protect himself from further hurt and disappointment by withdrawing somewhat from his wife and hope he can bury his pain in his job or other activities. When this happens, wives start complaining; never dreaming of the role they have played in making their husbands act this way.

So we need to get a whole lot better at understanding our men ... and how our words impact them! When you attack, criticize, blame, or complain – even if you aren't doing it intentionally – your man will feel like a loser ... or he'll have to fight to avoid feeling like a loser ... or he'll withdraw to avoid feeling like a loser ... all of which will leave him feeling ... like a loser. There's no way he can win. And, by the way, you can't win this way either.

Although he should never just do whatever you say – no matter how he thinks or feels about it, or how it affects his own self-worth – just to make you happy, he shouldn't tune you out either. We know that men in successful marriages are open to their wives' feedback. But when either person becomes a doormat, it creates different problems. You're a couple, dancing as one, remember? Both people matter.

Please believe me – and your guy – when we say that he really wants to see you actively, joyously happy ... especially with him. When that happens, you both win, and you both get to participate in the Dance of Romance. You win because you're happy, and he wins because he got something right. You won't believe what this does for a guy ... to be able to see his woman smile. So let's help him out, ladies. Let's help him know when he gets it right. But more about that in Chapter 8, "Home Improvement."

Conclusions

So men are different because of their nature and their nurture. They're sensitive, they speak a different language, and they are created with Divine Purpose. They are our Protectors, Providers, and Problem-solvers, and they want to Please us – to make us happy more than anything.

Shall we continue the Dance? Yes, let's!

Men Are Complicated

 *Chapter 6*

STAGES OF A MAN'S LIFE

Another way that men are different from us is in the course of their lifespan development. And where they are in the process of life will affect their Leadership capabilities, as well as the style of Dance they choose.

As those best suited to be Followers, women tend to be Adapters. That is, we can pretty much bloom wherever we're planted ... if we *want* to bloom, that is. (Yes. Mixed metaphors again.) We adapt to men, and we adapt to children. We adapt to our family of origin, and we adapt to the society in which we live. Whether we want to admit it or not, the course of female development is often highly dependent upon what's going for others.

For example, it's not unusual for a woman to obtain a college degree, build a career, then marry and have children. When the kids come along, a woman may take a break from her career or cut back on her hours in favor of being a mom.

It's also not unusual for a woman to marry young, help her husband through college, and forego her own degree and career until her children are older or out of the house.

Nor is it unusual for a woman to forego marriage to take care of an aging or ill parent or other family member. She may also join the military, fight in war, or run a business. For women, the possibilities seem endless.

Men adapt, too. But in general, their development is a bit more predictable ... a bit more linear. And with all the challenges that brings, they have even more reason to need women ... and for women to be really great at adapting.

During my studies at Christian universities, several professors drove home the idea that truth is truth. And that all truth is God's truth. That is, who God is and how He reveals Himself in His Creation cannot be in conflict with one another. If anything is true, it's because God created it, and it belongs to Him. All of it.

My professors explained the differences between *special revelation* and *general revelation*. Special revelation is Truth that is given us through the Word of God, whereas general revelation is available to anyone who bothers to take the time to observe His Creation. In brief, you don't have to be a Believer to observe God's truth in His Creation. You don't even have to be a psychologist! Go figure.

Nevertheless, several psychologists have proposed models of male development, and you can read about some of them in my book, *Mothers and Sons: How the Maternal Attachment Experience Affects Boys' Emotional and Social Development.* I could share that same information with you here, or I could offer you other models to consider. I could even review several non-psychologist approaches. There are many of each from which to choose.

However, I'm opting for a more light-hearted approach here, using men that are in my own life as examples. So my own developmental model includes the following four stages: Superhero, Adventurer, Hero, and King.

And again, I must caution that the following information *probably* applies to most men. There are always exceptions, so it will be up to you to check this part out for yourself ... to see if any of it applies to *your* man.

The Superhero

My grandson is the greatest. At this point, I actually have two grandsons, and they're both very awesome men-in-the-making. But only one is old enough to be my superhero ... so far.

All men want to be a hero – no matter how old they are. And, of course, it's really easy to do. At 4 years of age, my grandson had already figured out how to be my *Super*hero!

Depending on what day it was, he'd be Spider Man, Batman, or Superman – and he'd save me from the "mean guys" who lurked in the corner of my family room then sneaked up the stairs and into my walk-in closet. These villains would have gone undetected, but My Little Superhero knew they were there. He slung his web to capture them, then proudly announced that he had saved me, and I didn't have to be afraid anymore.

I remember the first time he saw me heading to a Saturday night dance. He stood back with the most delightful grin on his face as I descended the stairs. Totally fascinated, he watched intently as my skirt skimmed the steps behind me. "Gramma Debi," he sighed. "You look just like a Princess."

The most important work of boyhood is what he does for play ... pretending ... practicing for life and imagining the man that he wants to become. In acting out his dreams of manhood, my grandson created the most delightful story of "The Princess and the Superhero," which we played daily. And The Princess was me! ... unless his mom was around, that is. Then he had to choose. We'd give him a hard time of it, of course, and he adored having two women fight over him. What a great kid!

From the time boys are big enough to walk and to talk until they reach puberty, they engage in the serious business of acting out their ideas of what it means to be a man. They imitate their fathers, as well as what they see on television. It's always amazing and dramatic and larger than life. And it's a total joy to behold.

And it's often risky ... not that they're necessarily aware that it's risky ... but because it's fun and because it brings them so much pleasure. Boys also need freedom to explore ... to see what happens when you drop a raw egg off the front porch ... or put your salamander in a kitchen sink full of milk. It even makes sense – from his perspective – that he prove his ability to put an entire frog in his mouth.

Dancing With a Superhero

And while he's busy being a Superhero, he needs a Princess ... a woman who can imagine with him and who will join in his Dance of Play. FYI: There's still a boy inside every man ... even inside your grandpa! So always be ready to play!

However, our tendency as mothers, grandmothers, aunts, sisters, teachers, and babysitters may be to squelch his boyish explorations ... to make him act safe and sane ... when he's neither one ... and isn't supposed to be.

And no, he's not supposed to be clean all the time either. Number One Son could actually *create* dust, and he loved to collect rocks ... which were usually covered with dirt, of course. And he also collected bottle caps, which were both dirty *and* sticky. Ah, "The Joy of Life!" (So reads his high school yearbook ad ...)

Number Two Son appeared to be such a neat little guy, so his dirt could sneak up on you. We had an out-of-town guest for dinner one evening, and his father commented that he needed to wash his face. In his sweet little 3-year-old voice he said, "Why? Do I got some doi-ty on me?" Then he methodically lifted a dirty sock from his lap and wiped his mouth with it!

Before Number Three Son could even walk, he had a refined skill for getting dirty ... sort of like the character Pigpen in Charles Schultz's *Peanuts* cartoons. I'd always get everyone else ready, then dress him ... and he'd still manage to create a mess before we made it to the car.

We moved into a new house the summer he was three years old, and our new lawn was being seeded. (We lived in the Midwest, and most people didn't use sod in those days.) We had one section of the lawn where all the neighborhood boys would play with their toy trucks, and Number Three Son would get so covered with dirt that I'd have to turn the garden hose on him before I'd even let him in the house!

The Adventurer

Number Three Son married his college sweetheart, and their wedding programs contained pictures of them as children. What cute little blue-eyed blondes they both were! The photos that linger in my mind, however, were those taken when they were teenagers. My very pretty daughter-in-law sitting on a horse, complete with English riding gear. A very classy girl. And my son straddling his own trusty steed ... a motorcycle, of course. What is it about a child on a motorcycle that makes a mom nervous?

Once puberty strikes, a boy begins to connect his Superhero-self to Real Life Adventure. At this point, he's all about enjoying new experiences and mostly ... well, just having fun. Risky behavior abounds ... at least from Mom's point of view. Baseball, basketball, football, diving, and driving.

Secret treks to Who Knows Where and Don't Tell Mom. And doing things that only a boy's logic could imagine.

Which reminds me of Number Two Son – accidentally locking a friend's keys in the trunk of his car in the middle of the night at Someplace You're Not Supposed to Be and calling home with a lame excuse about why he was going to be late ... then getting caught red-handed anyway.

... And Number One Son – getting his car stuck in the mud at church in the middle of the night because he didn't want to walk across the field to the basketball goal and risk ruining the Nikes he'd borrowed from his roommate ... so he drove instead. It seemed like a good idea at the time.

That's just the tip of the Adventure Iceberg. It wouldn't be fair to tell it all, lest their own children find out what they were really like as teenagers. So enough said. It's pretty obvious that boys don't think like moms do. And I have to wonder: Why do so many of these adventures happen in the middle of the night? It's a wonder any of them make it through to adulthood!

Dancing With an Adventurer

Dancing with an Adventurer requires the ability to be a bona fide Adventuress. If you're not into it, you'll miss out on some of the best fun a girl can have. Guys who marry young will still be into adventure. It will pass ... at least in part. Some guys hang on to this stage as long as they can.

If this sounds like your man, you might want to read a book by John Eldredge – *Wild at Heart: Discovering the Secret of a Man's Soul*. Some men don't relate to his take on what it means to be a man, but it will give you another way of looking at the adventurer that – at some level – does exist in every man. That is to say that some guys aren't into the Great Outdoors, but they probably get excited about another brand of Adventure. It'll be up to you to watch for it.

The Hero

Heroes are everywhere. We just don't notice them. And therein lies the problem. Men love to be heroes, and they work very hard at it ... no matter how old they are. However, in terms of the stages of male development, a Hero is a man who has found his own Princess in Real Life and is in the process of building a career and family with her.

Unfortunately, this can be one of those Seasons that can create a Plethora of Problems for married couples. He's working hard to provide *for* his family, and she just wants him to spend time *with* his family. Both are very important, but they argue and arrive at Nowhere.

Dancing With a Hero

A Hero needs a partner, a Helpmate, for sure. So if you're dancing with a Hero, you'll need to get good at recognizing everything he's doing for you, even while you're assisting him in finding a balance between work, family, and play. The temptation is to nag ... to become his mom. Trust me, no guy wants to be married to his mom – no matter how wonderful he says she is!

If you're currently married to a Hero – and most of my counseling clients are – you may inadvertently be making matters worse – simply because you don't understand how his mind works. If he's building a career, it's probably deeply into One Track Mode. And if your Dance isn't going well, you'll want to be sure to pay particular attention to the information provided in Chapter 8, "What a Man Needs From a Woman," and Chapter 9, "Home Improvement."

The King

I used to think I could never fall in love with a middle-aged man. They all seemed so b-o-r-i-n-g ... and so o-l-d. (My sincere apologies to my middle-aged male friends.) And old guys seem to think they know everything ... so they always give you advice.

At this point, I've been pretty independent for a very long time. Plus, I'm still really young at heart, so I'd been thinking, "Give me a Hero who's still in the process ... and who still has a fair amount of the Superhero and the Adventurer in him. No, Sir-ee! No boring old guy for me!"

Boy, was I wrong! In the last year, I've learned that men who have already raised their families and/or established their careers are absolutely Wonderful! They are Kings! They know who they are, so you don't have to worry about them trying to prove themselves at your expense. Plus, they know what they like, as well as what they don't like, and they won't waste their time on anything they don't enjoy.

Although these men may still be unsure of themselves when it comes to women (especially if they're dancing single), they're fully aware of what they have to offer to women in general, and to their wives and children in particular.

And they give you advice ... not because they think you are stupid or wrong or incapable ... but because they want *you* to benefit from their experience! How sweet is that?

Dancing With a King

When you appreciate who he is and what he has to offer, you'll find that a King has absolutely the very best balance of Superhero, Adventurer, and Hero right there within him!

He needs a Dance Partner who accepts him just as he is, and who knows, understands, and respects his particular needs and desires. We'll turn to those soon, but first there's one more highly important issue we need to talk about ...

The Man Cave

An understanding of men necessarily includes a healthy respect for the Man Cave. But as women we typically have a really hard time with it. We have nothing to compare it to, so it simply doesn't make sense to us.

But it makes a lot of sense to men.

When we're worried about something, we usually want someone to walk and to talk though it with us. For the most part, our American culture has trained us to do just that.

However, the same culture has taught him to do the opposite! Remember the story of what typically happens to the toddler boy on the playground? Those early experiences were the beginning of his education in The Boy Code. He learned that a man has to appear tough – a Sturdy Oak – in order to be loved and respected. And he learned that a man must figure out his own problems and deal with all his vulnerable emotions – anger, sadness, fear, hurt, grief, shame, guilt, and doubt – on his own.

So that's what he does, and he does it in the Man Cave.

Looking at it from our side of the wall, the Man Cave feels like stonewalling at best and abandonment at worst. Simply knowing that her man is struggling is not enough, because that only serves to trigger a woman's natural desire to reach out and encourage him ... to get him to talk to her ... to try to convince him that she is his Safe Haven.

But a lifetime of experience has taught him otherwise. Her efforts to connect will feel like an invasion to him. And this invasion typically results in immediate defense – usually by strengthening his wall. And being shut out makes her more anxious ... worried about him ... and about herself. It feels like the Beginning of the End to her, and she often doesn't understand why. So she tries to fix it. But first she has to get through the wall. Drastic times call for drastic measures ... so she hauls out the Wrecking Ball.

You can see where this is going, right? Nowhere.

Absolutely Nowhere.

"So what do I do? I suppose you expect me to sit down on the curb outside the Man Cave and just wait for him to come out?" you ask in your frustration. "If I do that," you reason, "he'll never come out!"

Nope. There's so much more you can do to help him!

First, let him know you notice that something's up with him. And keep your remarks simple. You might say, "I feel like you're disappearing, and suspect that something's troubling you. Life is so hard on men. I don't know how you do it."

Second, shut up. Yes, I know I shouldn't tell you to "shut up" because my grandson told me those are "bad words." But it's *essential* that we learn this Important Fact:

> **When it comes to his emotions, something said in fewer words holds more meaning for a man.**

He listens in sentences, remember? So don't worry if he doesn't respond or offer more. Your empathy did register with him. And it made a difference. It made an immediate, significant difference. And by not probing him with a lot of questions or pounding him with further verbiage, you're demonstrating your respect for the Man Cave.

Third, if he does share his struggle, your job is simply to listen. He's testing the water to see if you're safe. You are. Your goal is to learn about him. No advice. No suggestions. Let your words be few and empathic (e.g., "sounds hard").

And, most importantly ... keep what he does share between you and the Lord.

Which brings us to the fourth and most important thing you can do. Pray for him. He doesn't necessarily need to know that you're praying, though some men do feel supported by that fact. If you tell him you're praying, say it once a day at most. And keep the content of your prayers between you and the Lord.

That's what he needs from you while he's in the Man Cave.

More on his needs in the next chapter ...

Chapter 7
WHAT A MAN NEEDS FROM A WOMAN

Oftentimes, a man in couples counseling will want to focus only on what will make his wife happy. That's very noble, and I love that about men. In fact, I've come to believe that *every* man's primary goal is to make his woman happy. And as I'm thinking about this now, I must confess that every man I've ever talked to about women has confirmed this as one of his Primary Life Goals: to make his woman happy.

So after a few counseling sessions, I ask the man how things went the previous week. He usually says, "It was better."

When I ask what was different – what made it better, his response is simple: "We didn't argue."

For him, that's progress. And it is for her, too.

But there's a lot more to it than that.

I remember one man in particular, a former Marine. We'd been talking for several weeks about various ways his wife wanted him to meet her emotional and relational needs. When I asked him what he needed from his wife, he smiled. "Nothing. I just want her to be happy."

Essay Question vs. Multiple Choice

This guy wasn't telling the whole story. But it's been my experience that men just aren't good at answering those essay-type questions. "What do you need from your wife?" feels like a blank page to him. And because he was raised to deny his own needs, he has a hard time recalling them.

However, men are great at recognizing the "right answer" when they hear it ... kind of like a multiple-choice test. As a former student and professor, I know those kinds of exams are easier on students and professors alike in that both enjoy less work than with the essay questions. The student merely needs to select the right answer ... it's right there in front of him. And the prof simply runs the Scantron through the machine, which makes grading a cinch.

So did I help the Marine out by giving him a multiple-choice question? No, not exactly. I affirmed what he'd just told me about his desire to make his wife happy, and how much it means to him to be able to be with her without the arguing.

Then I turned to his wife, restating what he'd said about not needing anything from her. She nodded and confirmed that he won't tell her what he needs either.

With a sense of hopelessness and confusion, she reported, "I ask him that all the time, and he always says, 'Nothing'."

I validated her experience and told her that the vast majority of men won't say what they need – and they do so for a variety of very good reasons. I told her what I've learned about men's needs. The Marine nodded – as most men do – as I provided a list of his needs for his wife. Then I gave him a chance to reply. "Yeah, that's it! That's exactly what I need." She gets it, and now both of them are happy. Ta da!

Let me share the list with you ...

The Most Important Factor

The first thing a man needs from his wife is evidence of her own self-confidence. So many times when things go wrong, we start trying to change ourselves. He picked you because he likes who you are.

As Billy Joel sings, "Don't go changing to try and please me. I love you just the way you are."

Here's an example: Cathy grew up dreaming of the perfect world. Pretty dresses. An elegant, well-situated Castle. And, of course, a Handsome Prince.

While they were dating, Mark fit the handsome-prince role perfectly. He was charming and thoughtful, and loved surprising Cathy with little gifts. And, of course, Christmas was the best! Everything he put under the tree for her was perfect – almost as though he'd kept detailed notes about all the things she had talked about throughout the year.

He certainly wasn't like her father, who never seemed to be around when she needed him. There was no doubt that her dad had always been a great Provider, working his way to the top of his company, but it had occupied most of his time and seemingly all of his energy.

For as long as Cathy could remember, her mother had complained that she felt like she'd been a single parent from the beginning. Yet for some reason, her mother seemed to blame herself for Dad's lack of involvement with the family. She was always upbeat, cajoling, trying to entice him to do things with the family. But it rarely worked.

Cathy felt it, too. It was as though she wasn't important to her dad. When she was a little girl, she tried her best to be cute and funny to get his attention. Sometimes it worked. Sometimes it didn't. She could never figure out why.

But Mark was so very different! At last Cathy had the male attention she had craved. Mark said – and demonstrated through his behavior – that his world revolved around her.

Reflecting on their first night in their new home after the honeymoon, Cathy remembered how shocked she was by Mark's sudden lack of responsiveness. All she had asked was that he turn off the TV so they could go to sleep. He'd acted as though he didn't even hear her!

So she turned on the charm. Nothing.

She became more vocal. Still no response.

Moving to the living room was her most dramatic ploy. She thought that would surely let him know she was upset and that he would follow her. But he didn't.

She had no idea what to do. Her sugar-and-spice routine had failed, and she couldn't figure out why. So she pulled away ... retreated, hoping Mark would feel guilty enough to follow her. He was such a wonderful man.

She *must* be doing something wrong. But what was it?

All these years later she still wonders what went wrong. She tried hard to make everything nice, but she failed miserably. And Mark felt like he had failed as well, though he never said as much. He only withdrew more and more as the years went by. Both of them got lost somehow.

Had Cathy known what was going on in Mark's mind, she might have approached the whole situation differently. And it would not have required emotional contortions and resorting to guilt and manipulation to get her needs met ... or his. In fact, Mark and Cathy might have both come out ahead of the game that night – a little more skilled in the Dance of Romance.

Another example comes from a question asked repeatedly by unmarried women. "We were getting along so well! I don't understand what happened. Why did he disappear? Did I do something wrong?"

Many single men tend to move forward in a relationship, then seem to back up – which can be a frustrating twist on the Country Two-Step for the women they've expressed an interest in. Some women take it all in stride, whereas others begin to struggle with their self-confidence. And we know that women with low self-confidence can be very, very unattractive to men. Which can lead to that old, inevitable self-fulfilling prophecy about being unlovable.

So what's a woman to do? Some decide to "fake it 'til you make it." So do you pretend to be something you're not? Seriously. How can that be helpful?

Others say "dump the dude!" … But isn't that like quitting before you get fired? So do you pursue him? No, that never works. It's very unflattering to say the least.

Time for a reality check.

First of all, whenever a man appears to be taking a step back from a relationship, that may or may not be the reality. Remember that men don't think or behave like a woman, so there's absolutely no point in judging him according to the standards of the Ideal Woman. He may just be busy.

He may also be taking a relational time out … and thinking about where he needs to lead next. If he truly cares about you, he'll give your relationship a lot of thought and prayer. Being a Leader in the Dance of Romance is an awesome task that can feel overwhelming. A good man will want to get it right. So he may need to spend some time in the Man Cave.

And it may not be something you need to figure out right now. Let the Lord do that for you. In a word, pray.

Although it's true that a woman's self-esteem relies heavily on what she thinks her man thinks of her, it shouldn't rule her life. Your self-esteem and your self-confidence must be based on the unconditional love of Christ.

If you're a Christian, reconnect with Jesus daily ... if not moment-by-moment (1 Thessalonians 5:17). And if you've not yet accepted Him as your Savior, you are invited to do so right now. He's right there with you ... wherever you are in the process of life ... eagerly waiting to hear from you!

Having Jesus in your heart makes all the difference in the world! You can place your full confidence in His love for you. In the words of songwriter Tim Timmons,

> Jesus you lavished on me
> Your revolutionary love love love
> Love love love
> I am Your masterpiece
> Created for the world to see see see
> Your love love love through me

As you grasp the reality of God's love for you, you'll realize you can fully trust Him to take care of and guide you. And if the guy really is going away, it's probably for your best.

Needy or Openly Vulnerable?

The second thing a man needs from a woman is her honesty about who she is in terms of her own vulnerability. In other words, a Real Man needs a Real Woman to dance with.

Neediness gets such a bum rap. As one of my mentors told me, "To say that someone is too needy is like saying they are too human." And he was right. We are all *very* needy. We absolutely cannot survive very long without one another ... or a facsimile thereof. Do you remember "Wilson," Tom Hanks's volleyball friend in the movie *Castaway*? Human contact is so essential that we will create a face into which we can gaze. Animal, vegetable, or mineral, we derive great comfort in believing that we are not alone.

So if nothing is wrong with being needy, why are so many men so turned off by it? My guess is that it has nothing to do with any lack of empathy. Most men are *wonderfully* empathic. However, inexplicable emotion quickly becomes difficult for most of them because they can't figure out what the problem is – what it is that you need, what they can do to help. So like in the movie *Jerry McGuire*, he might say, "Help me help you."

So let's go with vulnerability. By all means, do tell him how you feel. Just be brief and specific. It's also okay to cry, as long as you give him something to do that will help you feel better. This is definitely one of those times when "even guys with two left feet come out alright if the girl is sweet."

A word of caution is needed here. Be sure you're honestly sharing your needs, concerns, or feelings, and not that you're moving into manipulation or guilt or attempting to fix whatever you think is wrong with him. We'll talk about how to help him become a better man in Chapter 8. But for now ... let's keep working on you ...

Have a Life of Your Own

Guys love to give to us, but interestingly enough, they're most inclined to be there for us when we don't seem like we need them. That's a confusing comment, even to me, and I'm the one who just wrote it! But it's true. If you're passionate about your life, he'll naturally work harder to find ways to contribute to your life. He'll want to be a part of your life because you make his brain fire in the most delightful of ways. He won't say that, of course. But you'll know because of how much likes to be around you.

No, this is not manipulation. We really *do* need to get a life of our own ... something that God has called us to do ... our unique contribution to His Kingdom. You'll feel the energy, and so will he! It will draw him to you just like a moth to a flame. In fact, your passion will inspire *many* men to want to help – the kid bagging your groceries, your dentist, and even your grandpa. And there's a bonus if he happens to be a love interest (e.g., husband, possible husband) in that he'll also see your passion for life as Totally Hot! ;)

Do You Wanna Dance With *Me*?

I've heard it said that there's a reason why bridegrooms are all dressed alike ... Because it doesn't really matter what man you plug in to the role. It's only the bride that counts. The man just isn't that important.

You may chuckle about that, but it feels true to many men.

A woman is frequently surprised if she hears that her man feels like he's simply not that important to her ... that he doesn't believe he's very high on her list of priorities. In fact, he might feel like he's not even *on* her list! He may believe that he's nothing more than a paycheck to her ... something to be used up by her. And he doesn't want sex in exchange for his paycheck. He honestly wants to feel emotionally *connected* to her, but he just can't figure out how to make it happen.

Yes, he knows you want to dance, but he may be having a really hard time believing that it's *him* you want to be dancing with!

There are so many ways men try to connect with us ... to ask us to dance with them.

And it requires a tremendous amount of courage to ask ... especially if they have been shot down a lot.

However, each time a man gets a "yes," he's encouraged to ask again ... and again ... and again ...

Here are just a few essential ways that you can say "yes" to the men in your life ...

#1. Your Attention

Men are only interested in *one* thing? Well, it's not sex.

Yes, it's true that sex with his wife is *one thing* that makes a man feel loved. But, what he wants most is your attention.

In fact, he's always needed a woman's attention.

Like most boys, all three of my sons were involved in sports. Swimming, soccer, baseball, basketball, football, and cross country. And one of the most important predictors of their enjoyment was whether or not mom was there to watch.

For example, as a little guy in his first swimming lessons, Number One Son stood there on the diving board shouting, "Mom! Mom!" to be sure I was watching before he'd jump. And just as soon as his little head bobbed out of the pool, he'd look in my direction and wait for his well-deserved cheer. Then back to the diving board for another plunge ... and more smiles from Mom!

Men don't change much in this regard. They crave female attention. Your attention will be especially important if he's a love interest (e.g., husband or possible husband).

Look at him adoringly when he talks to you. Listen intently to what he has to say. Why? Because every time he speaks, he's sharing something about who he is – his thoughts, his beliefs, his hopes, his fears, his values. Men share far more than we realize, but they do it differently than we do. And if he believes you're interested, he'll keep talking.

On the other hand, if you interrupt, interject, or make it about you, he'll assume you're just not into what he's saying and will stop talking. We do this far more often than we realize we do because of our female communication style. What to do then?

Be a safe person for him. Don't evaluate what he says or compare him to yourself or to another man. Don't probe or ask questions, unless you're simply saying, "Tell me more." And don't share intimate details with your girlfriends.

#2. Your Acceptance

My Superhero grandson was only three when he moved to California – with his parents, of course. And he loved going for leisurely walks around the neighborhood with me. Always drawn to flowers, he had to stop and smell each one along the way. I instructed him that we mustn't pick them because they belonged to my neighbors. So he'd patiently remind me as he admired their bright colors and imagined fragrance, "We can't pick your neighbor's flowers."

However, he didn't apply the same rule to flowers blooming in front of the bank or in the park or next to Carl's Jr. He'd race over and pick one as soon as he saw them, then present it to me with a gigantic smile on his sweet little face.

"Here! This is for you, Gramma!" he'd announce with great pleasure, fully expecting my reflected joy for the gift he so proudly bestowed. Of course, I was always very delighted … and I refrained from shaming him for picking the flower.

Men don't change in this regard either. Remember they still love to make us smile. No matter his age, whenever he sees you smile, it brightens his day … and his life!

You don't have to pretend that he's perfect, or that his gifts are perfect. When you accept what he brings to your life, you are accepting him. And that's a very good thing.

So the best response is very simple: Say "thank you" with a smile on your face. You'll make his day.

Have you ever responded to your guy's gift with some sort of critique? He "wasted" money on flowers. You'd rather have such-and-such. Why didn't he _____ (fill in the blank)?

If you do that to him again and again, he'll be inclined to give up the possibility of making you happy. And at some point, he won't even try anymore.

Remember that your man wants to be your hero – always. God designed him with a natural desire to protect you, to guide you, and to hold you – to make you happy – if you'll only let him. He won't do it perfectly. So you will need to let go of your tendency to correct him, to teach him, to give him advice – even about how to dance. Those messages tell him he's not good enough – that he will never be good enough – and that he'll never be able to make you happy.

#3. Your Affection

Several years ago, I read about an experiment that was conducted somewhere in the restaurant business. These researchers were exploring the value of touch in human interactions. Servers in the control group went about their work as usual, whereas servers in the experimental group were instructed to briefly touch their customer's hand while in the process of serving the food. The independent variable was *touch*, and the dependent variable was *the amount of the tip* the customer left for the server.

Guess what? Those servers who touched their customer's hand received much higher tips!

Seriously. Like we didn't see that coming?

We are all so hungry for human touch, and we rarely get that need met. Women, of course, have a better shot at it because it's more socially acceptable for them to hug one another. But we do more than just hug. We actually hold one another.

Q: Do you know the difference between *hugging* someone and *holding* them?

A: About 10 seconds.

But after a certain age, men are rarely held ... unless they're having sex. Perhaps that's what makes sex so essential for a man's sense of well-being?

In fact, a number of forty-something husbands have said, "She never touches me anymore."

That's so sad ... especially when you realize that their wives want to be touched as well. I'm not talking about sexual touch, and neither are these men. They're talking about day-to-day, nonsexual, incidental touch ... an amazingly powerful connection with your partner.

So when dinner's ready tonight, don't holler at him to come and eat. Go to wherever he is and stand beside him, place your hand on his shoulder or arm, then smile and softly say, "Dinner's ready."

Then turn and walk away quietly. Even if he doesn't move a muscle or say a word ... or even come and eat ... you can be sure your touch and soft voice registered in his brain.

There's nothing more calming than making contact with the person you love most. So make physical contact as often as you can. You don't have to be dramatic about it. Start slow. Remember, his brain will notice even if he doesn't.

And if he's in the mood for sex, take it as a positive indicator ... that he needs to be held ... by you.

#4. Your Appreciation

A simple "Thank You" goes a long, long way.

Enough said? Yes, I believe it is.

And now on to the Chapter you've been waiting for ...

 *Chapter 8*

HOME IMPROVEMENT

You've probably heard the saying that when a man marries a woman he's hoping she'll never change, whereas a woman marries a man hoping that he will. It's actually more than a hope for her. He may actually be her Main Project.

But men are not projects. They are people.

I don't like to be the bearer of bad tidings, ladies, but God only created one perfect man so far ... and it's taken Him nearly 60 years to refine him. On the Brightside, however, if the Lord is doing such a great job on this one, I believe He can do the same with your guy! Your man can be so much more, and you can actually help him become *Your* Fearless Leader in the Dance of Romance!

Simply put, it's a woman's job to love her man and pray for him. It's God's job to make him grow ... and according to His plan, not hers. Your man wants to be your Leader in the Dance of Romance ... to protect you and to guide you and to hold you ... to choreograph the Dance to maximize your pleasure in being with him.

But much of the time we're shooting ourselves in the foot by doing all the things that *don't work* to change him ... instead of doing things that *do work* to change him … things that he actually *wants* you to do to shape his behavior! Go figure.

What Doesn't Work?

Before we know what works, we must learn what doesn't. So our free "Prelude to a Dance" seminars for women in Newport Beach always start with this fill-in-the blank:

> * The thing that troubles me most about men is
> _____.

Then we discuss all the ways we've tried to change whatever it is we don't like about them. None of it has ever worked, of course, but don't we keep doing the same thing over and over again, expecting different results? Wait! Isn't that the textbook definition of "crazy?" Yes, I believe it is!

There are several strategies that women try repeatedly in their attempts to change a man. Here's a very brief list of some of the things we've all tried … at one time or another … and the reasons why they don't work.

Hints

In plain, simple language: "Guys don't do hints." Why not? Because they don't even recognize them! Hints are clouded with Girl Code, which they can't even being to comprehend. So why rely so heavily on hints when they never work?

We hint that we'd like to go out to eat … or to Hawaii. Our word choices can be so vague that men are often left in the dark about what it is we're saying … or that we were even saying anything of significance at all!

We say, "Notice anything new?" Which is as dangerous as, "Does this outfit make me look fat?" It feels like a setup to him … like a trap … especially if past conversations have resulted in your anger. Of course, we know that your anger comes from having your feelings hurt. So why not avoid that probability altogether ... by setting him up to win right from the start?

One poor husband was painfully unaware of what his wife needed and wanted or even what she liked! He wanted so badly to please her, but he kept tripping over himself in the process. We were talking about their sexual relationship in one very tearful session, and I asked his wife to share with him just one thing that she liked.

She refused and said with an angry tone, "No, I'm not going to tell him. I shouldn't have to tell him. He should just know. If I tell him, then he'll do it, but only because I told him to, not because he wants to."

So her expectation was that he should read her mind? The last I knew, men and women dwell in very different bodies with very different designs. What's pleasurable to one is not necessarily the most enjoyable for the other. How can he possibly know unless she tells him? ... And just exactly what's wrong with him doing something that he knows would bring her pleasure?

Having said that, I really do understand her struggle. Most women are at least a little ambivalent about their sexuality. However, life is so much easier when we're direct. I know we weren't brought up that way, but sometimes we need to acquire new skills ... and new confidence ... in ourselves and in our partner.

Criticism

Women respond to criticism. It changes us. For example, I was wearing my favorite periwinkle blue blouse one day, and another woman told me that I really don't look good in that color. Now I happen to know for a fact that periwinkle blue is actually one of my very *best* colors. It makes my eyes appear more blue than they already are ... and they are already pretty darn blue. No, I've not stopped wearing that blouse. But I do make note of what I'm planning to wear on the days I know I'll be seeing her.

"How crazy is that?" you ask.

Pretty darn. But it's what we women do.

Men don't operate that way. Criticism only serves to rally their defensiveness, so it has the opposite effect on them. They'll go ahead and do it anyway ... or avoid the person ... or hide what they're doing.

One thing is sure: Criticizing a man will backfire every time.

Comparison

Many of us – but certainly not all – care way too much about what others are thinking of us ... probably because we're constantly judging one another.

Our standard: our concept of the Ideal Woman. Of course, none of us can measure up to that! And then we expect a *man* to measure up to the Ideal Woman?

"How crazy is that?" I ask.

Pretty darn. But it's what we women do.

Comparing our man to the Ideal Woman ... or to *anyone* ... is crazy. He's unique, and God loves him right now ... right where he is ... exactly the way he is. And if Our Holy God loves him, how can we dare to think we have a better idea? Honestly. We have neither the wisdom nor the power to change ourselves for the better, much less improve on a man ... for whom we have no blueprint in the first place.

Nagging

It makes him feel like a little boy. Which makes you feel like his mom. Not helpful for either of you. Enough said. There is a better way, but first ...

A Word (or Two) About Manipulation, Drama, and Guilt

A woman's good opinion should never be bestowed lightly or insincerely. When you pay him a compliment, it should be a totally honest one. Flattery is cheap and manipulative. Any woman who wants to improve her relationship must avoid manipulation and drama at all costs. Walk away from them both. Drama will drain him ... and you, eventually.

Guilt trips are our specialty. We learn them from our moms. If you're not sure what one looks like, watch any episode of "Everybody Loves Raymond." Marie Barone is the Queen! Very funny on TV. Not so much in real life.

So what's the best way to improve your chances of getting your needs met? Ask for what you want ... be specific and concrete ... and accept his response whether it's *yes* or *no*.

Many women seem to be unaware of which behaviors might come across to others as manipulation, drama, or guilt. So ask your best friend – or a trusted counselor – to help you become aware of the times and situations in which you are most likely to engage in any of these tactics. Then cut it out.

What Does Work?

Clearly, a lot of our strategies don't work.

"So does anything work to change a man?" you ask.

Yes, and I'm so excited that I finally figured it out, and I can hardly wait to share it with you! Here's what I've learned ... and how I introduce it to the women who come to my office for help with Home Improvement (also known as *Husband* Improvement).

At some point in couples counseling, I will say to the man, "Don't listen to this part."

Then I turn to his lady and let her in on His Best Kept Secret, "Men are like small children and dogs. If they are beaten or shamed for bad behavior, it just makes them avoid us. They may even cower when we come near.

"On the other hand, if we focus on what they do *right* and reward them for it, they'll go out of their way to get that reward again and again and again."

By this time, the man – although he's not listening – begins to smile and nod enthusiastically. "Ya!!! Do that!!!"

It's predictable. I have yet to hear a man say he's offended by my suggestion that his wife should treat him like a dog. And no wonder! Most women are kinder to their pets than they are to the man they love. How odd is that?

Think about it. You're happy to see your dog at the end of a long day, and you make sure Rover knows it. You talk to him sweetly and scratch him behind his ear. You take time to pet him and make sure he's fed. You even take him for a walk. And when he's a "Good Boy," you reward him with even more attention!

So there's really only one way to change a man:
Positive Reinforcement

The real, scientific definition of *reinforcement* is anything that *increases* the likelihood that a *target behavior* will occur again.

In our case, the *target behavior* is anything that he does that makes us feel loved, cared for, and respected.

And reinforcement can be *positive* or *negative*. So at least in theory, both types of reinforcement increase the likelihood that the target behavior will occur again.

Negative reinforcement means that something unpleasant is taken away. For example, whenever you take an aspirin (*target behavior*) to deal with a headache, your headache will go away (*negative reinforcement*). Therefore, the next time a headache hits, it's more likely that you'll take an aspirin again ... because doing so the last time resulted in negative reinforcement. Or your man finally takes out the trash (*target behavior*), and your constant nagging goes away (*negative reinforcement*). So – at least in theory – the next time you start nagging, it's more likely he'll take out the trash because the last time resulted in negative reinforcement. But, that last example backfires sometimes, doesn't it? He may just learn to tune you out, which also ends the nagging ... and your relationship as you would like it to be.

I don't know about you, but headaches and nagging are not what I would want *my* man to have fresh on his mind whenever he thinks of me!

Reinforcement can also be positive in that something can be added, such as your "thank you" or your smile. He does something nice. You smile and say, "Thank you." Through positive reinforcement, you just increased the likelihood that he'll do something nice again.

So he does something nice yet again. So you smile and say, "Thank you." Now we've really got something good going!

In reality, that's the way it was in the beginning of your relationship. But most of us stop saying "Thank you" and begin to expect – rather than hope for and appreciate – good things from our guys.

Yes, it really is that easy to change a man ... for the better. But it took me years – and the advice of one great guy – to be able to put two and two together. I am a blonde, after all.

If I'd only paid attention sooner I could have figured it out way back when I was completing all those undergraduate studies. And I could have skipped grad school altogether ...

I missed the obvious when I was in charge of the Rat Lab in the Undergraduate Psychology Department at MidAmerica Nazarene University. During my senior year, I had the privilege to work with Dr. Arvin Oke on an experiment that won a Psi Chi Regional Research Award, and attended the Southwest Psychological Association Convention that spring in Houston, Texas, with a poster presentation of our work. The title of our project was "Selective Attention Dysfunction in Rats Treated With 6-Hydroxy Dopamine." Don't ask.

The first step in the experiment was to teach my baby rats to perform in a maze using a process called *shaping*. By rewarding them for *successive approximations* of the target behavior (their treat was just a tiny bit farther away each time), before long, these amazing little creatures had learned to sprint down the maze, select the correct sign, then open the door to collect their prize. A complex task for sure!

I didn't give my baby rats hints, nor did I criticize, compare, nag, or resort to manipulation, drama, and guilt when they made mistakes. None of that would have worked.

I was just very consistent in dispensing their rewards. After awhile, they performed the target behavior without a treat. But the treat made them so happy that I always gave it to them anyway. Why not?

Hmm. I wonder what men think of the Rat Lab example. I don't think I want to know!

All that matters is ... that it is, indeed, possible to change a man. And he'll love you all the more for doing it. After all, his goal is to make you happy, remember? You just need to let him know when he's succeeded!

Part 4
The Sweethearts Ball

LEARNING TO DANCE AS ONE

Let Me Call You Sweetheart

I am dreaming Dear of you, day by day
Dreaming when the skies are blue,
When they're gray;
When the silv'ry moonlight gleams,
Still I wander on in dreams,
In a land of love, it seems,
Just with you.

Let me call you "Sweetheart," I'm in love with you.
Let me hear you whisper that you love me too.
Keep the love-light glowing in your eyes so true.
Let me call you "Sweetheart," I'm in love with you.

Longing for you all the while, more and more;
Longing for the sunny smile I adore;
Birds are singing far and near,
Roses blooming ev'rywhere
You alone my heart can cheer; You, just you.

~ Leo Friedman (music)
~ Beth Slater Whitson (lyrics)
published in 1910

The Sweethearts Ball shows the unparalleled beauty of the Romantic Dance between a man and a woman in a very powerful way.

First, make sure you're dancing to the right music. Not the music of this world. Dance to the Heavenly Music provided by Your Creator.

Also realize that no man was born knowing how to lead, and no woman was born knowing how to follow. It's a lifelong process in which Grace and Forgiveness are continually required.

Be attuned to one another and – most important of all – never leave your partner behind!

Chapter 9

DANCE TO THE BEST MUSIC

There's nothing sweeter than watching a couple in love. And if they happen to be dancing, it's all the more beautiful. And there's nothing more delightful than the experience of dancing with the perfect partner. The man who knows how to lead his lady (gently and confidently) dancing with the one woman who adores him and knows how to follow him (without losing who she is) is indeed a joy to behold.

The Melody you choose ensures the Sweetness of the Dance!

In order to create a beautiful Romantic Dance, you must be sure you're dancing to the most beautiful of melodies. Make sure you're attuned to Heaven … that is, responsive both to God and to one another. At its core, Romance is really about intimate connection with Our Heavenly Father, as well as with one another. In fact, we might want apply the following verse to both relationships:

> *My beloved is mine and I am his.*
> ~ Song of Solomon 2:16a

Marriage expert Dr. Susan Johnson puts it this way,

> *When marriages fail, it is not increasing conflict that is the cause. It is decreasing affection and emotional*

responsiveness, according to a landmark study by Ted Huston of the University of Texas. Indeed, the lack of emotional responsiveness rather than the level of conflict is the best predictor of how solid a marriage will be five years into it. The demise of marriages begins with a growing absence of responsive intimate interactions. The conflict comes later. (p. 38)

Life's a dance you learn as you go. It's really about learning to stay connected. Despite our romantic fantasies, life isn't just one never-ending waltz. Nor is it a never-ending polka.

Sometimes one ... or both ... of us will need to sit down and rest. And resting is also part of the dance.

Truly my soul finds rest in God;
my salvation comes from him. ~ Psalm 62:1

"Come to me, all you who are weary and burdened,
and I will give you rest." ~ Matthew 11:28

If you're a man, most of the time you'll lead. But sometimes you'll be sick or tired or discouraged or penniless, and will need your partner to be there for you. Sometimes she won't be able to dance, and you'll need to carry her because she's sick or tired or discouraged or penniless. That's how life goes. Most importantly ... Stay connected no matter what!

Emotion and Reason

God gave men *and* women both the capacities to feel and to reason, so they must be important things for each of us to have in our possession. And we need to learn to use them in balance. We need to be balanced within ourselves, and when we're not, we need our loving partner to help us find the balance again.

That's one of the reasons God designed us to live in pairs ... for balance. Pretty cool, eh?

Emphasis: One partner doesn't get to operate only by reason and the other operate only by emotions. We have both been given both, and both are to use both.

Heavenly Melody or Clanging Cymbal?

One of the ways you can evaluate your music is by looking at the results of your communication. During the course of his studies on marriage, Dr. John Gottman noticed that partners continually made "bids" for one another's attention, closeness, and reassurance through comments, questions, and/or gestures.

In successful marriages, spouses responded positively to these bids 86% of the time. Through their words and their actions, they invited more connection. They communicated – with or without words – the thoughts, "You matter to me" and "I want to connect with you, too."

In fact, successful couples offered at least 20 (yes, twenty) positive responses for every 1 (one) negative response!

So if you are dancing to a Heavenly Melody, you should be getting – and giving – a positive response about 86% of the time. That's like batting 860! A pretty hefty average, eh?

However, if you recognize any of the following tendencies in your communication, you may be hearing and dancing to a Clanging Cymbal:

1. **Harsh comments:** When your bids for your partner's attention start with a harsh comment, there's a 94% chance you won't get a positive response! Go figure.
2. **Criticism:** You usually know when you're being critical. Other times, you may assume you're just engaging in playful sarcasm. Although you may be joking, it's never a good idea to launch *any* kind of attack on your partner by questioning his or her character, intelligence, and/or abilities – especially in front of friends and family – even in jest.

3. **Generalized statements:** Such as "You never ...," "You always ...," or "What's wrong with you?"
4. **Stonewalling:** Withdrawing and/or refusing to respond to your partner when you're hurt definitely won't get either of you anywhere.
5. **Defensiveness:** Assuming your partner is going to be critical from the start can set you up for reactively attacking in self-protection. Instead, assume that not everything he or she says is meant as an attack. Your partner may be trying to tell you something important, but just be really bad at letting you know what he or she needs or wants. Be patient and listen.
6. **Contempt:** This is particularly toxic. Couples who show contempt for one another – either verbally or nonverbally – rarely get the love they want.

If any of this sounds all too familiar to you, please don't despair. Each of these are learned behaviors that contradict God's Word, and they can be unlearned. Always remember that help is available. Find a well-trained Christian counselor to assist you and your partner in getting out of the negative cycle. It can be done! I see it happen in my office all the time, and I can tell you for sure that it works best when both partners are following Christ and praying for one another on a regular basis. Love never gives up!

Forgiveness Is Our Only Option

At one time or another, we hurt the ones we love – whether we mean to or not. Sometimes we're just being selfish – totally self-absorbed, and we don't even realize the level of pain our actions will cause for our spouses. Whatever the reason, it simply shouldn't happen – in a perfect world.

But we don't live in a perfect world. We live in a fallen world. We are all fallible. And we all need forgiveness. And as Christians, we are *required* to forgive one another. Why? Because Jesus said so.

"For if you forgive other people when they sin against you, your heavenly Father will also forgive you. But if

you do not forgive others their sins, your Father will not forgive your sins." ~ Matthew 6:14-15

Even so, we all have the ability – and tendency – to harbor resentment. It's the human way – that is, it's our natural bent. We want to get even. To punish the one who hurt us. Yes, you can decide not to forgive. But is that *really* what you want to do?

Seeing God in Your Spouse

At my church back home, we used to sing,

> I love you with the love of God.
> I can see Him in you,
> the Glory of Our King.
> I love you with the love of God.

Is that what you're thinking when you say "I love you" to your spouse? Dan Allender and Tremper Longman said it well in their book *Intimate Allies*:

> *Marriage is the soil for growing glory. We must see our spouses in light of what they are meant to become, without turning bitter or complacent about who they are. Marriage requires a radical commitment to love our spouses as they are, while longing for them to become what they are not yet. Every marriage moves either toward enhancing one another's glory or toward degrading each other.* (p. 11)

Whether we're male or female, our role in marriage is neither to control nor to fix our spouses. We are expected to love them *just as they are* and *long for the best* for them. To long for something means to have an earnest or strong desire or craving for it. What a comforting thought that is!

> My partner *loves me* just as I am ... and *longs for me* to become what I am not yet ... and only in accordance with God's plan for me.

What does your dance look like? Are you enhancing one another's glory? Are you determined to learn to be adept at making your partner look good to anyone who's watching? ... and at believing God to do His best work in him or her?

Never Leave Your Partner Behind

Being a partner with a partner who's following Jesus means you're both heading in the same direction. Just don't leave one another behind on the Dance floor!

In the movie *Fireproof*, the motto of the Fire Department was "Never leave your partner behind." Caleb (Kirk Cameron) learned to apply the same motto to his marriage. Being a Hopeful Romantic who enjoys quoting lines from romantic movies, I often refer to members of a couple as "partners" during counseling ... and to this line from one of my all-time favorite movies.

By definition, a partner is someone who takes part with another. The dictionary also provides a list of synonyms for our consideration. Pick a few favorites ...

Accomplice	Comrade	Mate
Ally	Confederate	Pal
Assistant	Consort	Participant
Associate	Coworker	Playmate
Buddy	Crony	Sidekick*
Chum	Date	Spouse
Cohort	Friend	Teammate
Collaborator	Helper	Wife
Colleague	Helpmate	
Companion	Husband	

* This one's my personal just-for-fun favorite.

Bottom line: *Love Is the More Excellent Way.*

At our most recent Couples Workshop, we enjoyed dancing to a beautiful musical arrangement of 1 Corinthians 13, recorded by the Women's Choir at Azusa Pacific University.

Love is the More Excellent Way ...

If I speak in the tongues of men or of angels, but do not have love, I am only a resounding gong or a clanging cymbal. If I have the gift of prophecy and can fathom all mysteries and all knowledge, and if I have a faith that can move mountains, but do not have love, I am nothing. If I give all I possess to the poor and give over my body to hardship that I may boast, but do not have love, I gain nothing.

Love is patient, love is kind. It does not envy, it does not boast, it is not proud. It does not dishonor others, it is not self-seeking, it is not easily angered, it keeps no record of wrongs. Love does not delight in evil, but rejoices with the truth. It always protects, always trusts, always hopes, always perseveres.

Love never fails. But where there are prophecies, they will cease; where there are tongues, they will be stilled; where there is knowledge, it will pass away. For we know in part and we prophesy in part, but when completeness comes, what is in part disappears. When I was a child, I talked like a child, I thought like a child, I reasoned like a child. When I became a man, I put the ways of childhood behind me. For now we see only a reflection as in a mirror; then we shall see face to face. Now I know in part; then I shall know fully, even as I am fully known.

And now these three remain: faith, hope and love. But the greatest of these is love.

~ 1 Corinthians 13

Dance to the Best Music

Chapter 10

LEARNING TO LEAD

You remember Adam and Eve, right? They were the first couple, and they had it made. Then they got themselves into Big Trouble. Everyone knows Eve started the whole thing. She was deceived by the serpent, and she ate the forbidden fruit. Then she encouraged her husband to eat as well. But she wasn't who God came looking for, was she?

"Adam, where are you?"

Like it or not, the buck still stops here ... with you. I am constantly amazed by the weight of responsibility you guys carry on a day-to-day basis. And most of you do it with style and grace. But it's a struggle. I understand that ... more than you will ever realize. My goal is to help your wife understand that, too.

I often recommend that women watch the movies *Fireproof* and *Courageous* because if a picture's worth a thousand words, then a great movie is worth a million more.

One of my favorite movie scenes is in *Superman: The Movie*. Lois Lane (Margot Kidder) is holding on tight to a strap, the only thing that's keeping her from falling to her death from the News helicopter that's hanging precariously off the side of the Daily Planet building in Metropolis. Her yellow hat drifts to the ground and lands right in front of Clark Kent (Christopher Reeve). He looks up and springs into action. Without a proper phone booth in sight – anyone remember those? – he spins around in the nearest revolving door and emerges as Superman.

Just as Lois's strength gives out and she begins her rapid descent, Superman swoops up to catch her.

"Don't worry. I've got you," he says gently and confidently.

Lois looks at him in amazement, then down at the ground, then back at her rescuer. "You've got *me*? Who's got *you*?"

Good question. All too often women expect men to be as invincible as Supermen, forgetting that they are human, too.

The words of the song "Lead Me" by Sanctus Real provide another – more true-to-life – expression of the pressure you men feel as our leaders ... and emphasize your desperate need for God's help to be the leader He wants you to be.

> I look around and see my wonderful life
> Almost perfect from the outside
> In picture frames I see my beautiful wife
> Always smiling
> But on the inside, I can hear her saying ...
>
> "Lead me with strong hands
> Stand up when I can't
> Don't leave me hungry for love
> Chasing dreams, but what about us?
>
> Show me you're willing to fight
> That I'm still the love of your life
> I know we call this our home
> But I still feel alone"
>
> I see their faces, look in their innocent eyes
> They're just children from the outside
> I'm working hard, I tell myself they'll be fine

They're independent
But on the inside, I can hear them saying ...

"Lead me with strong hands
Stand up when I can't
Don't leave me hungry for love
Chasing dreams, but what about us?

Show me you're willing to fight
That I'm still the love of your life
I know we call this our home
But I still feel alone"

So Father, give me the strength
To be everything I'm called to be
Oh, Father, show me the way
To lead them

Won't You lead me?
To lead them with strong hands
To stand up when they can't
Don't want to leave them hungry for love,
Chasing things that I could give up

I'll show them I'm willing to fight
And give them the best of my life
So we can call this our home
Lead me, 'cause I can't do this alone

Father, lead me, 'cause I can't do this alone

God First

Without a doubt, the First Thing you need to be the Leader
you want to be is Jesus. He is absolutely The Essential One,
not only for your well-being, but also for your family's well-
being. If you're a Christian, reconnected with Him daily ...
if not moment-by-moment (1 Thessalonians 5:17). If you've
not yet accepted him as your Savior, you can do so right
now. He's right there with you ... wherever you are in the
process of life, and He's eagerly waiting to hear from you!

Take Advantage of Your Wife ... in a Good Way

Here are a few ways for you enjoy the benefits of marriage ... receiving the love and moral support that you also need to be able to lead well ...

- Listen to her.
- Be her hero (i.e., treat her like a lady).
- Pay attention to how she's responding to your leadership.
- Ask for what you need from her ... that's in addition to a great sex life, of course.
- Be strong enough to allow yourself to be vulnerable with her.

If you're finding yourself stuck on any of these points, or if you think of anything else I can help you with, please do let me know. I look forward to hearing from you, whether you have a question, something to share, or encouragement to offer. I welcome it all!

Bottom Line: *My goal is to help men and women find better ways of relating to and enjoying one another, so I'm always looking for more opportunities to spread the Good News.*

I met a new couple at my church recently and was sharing about my specialty as a psychologist. I told them I teach classes for women about the psychology of men, and that we women often don't really get men. The guy immediately turned to his girlfriend and said, "I'll pay for you to go to her classes." He was totally serious.

At the end of each of my presentations, I encourage women to go home, sit down, and have a talk with their men. I tell them to share what they've heard from me and to ask their guys whether or not the information applies to them. The feedback I get is that men believe that I actually do get them. But I'm still a woman, so I know I don't get it right every time. Just ask the men who know me. Eh, guys?

Bottom Line: *Your* woman is going to love the experience of following a godly man who knows how to lead gently and confidently. It's unforgettable joy!

> Unforgettable, that's what you are
> Unforgettable though near or far
> Like a song of love that clings to me
> How the thought of you does things to me
> Never before has someone been more
>
> Unforgettable in every way
> And forever more, that's how you'll stay
> That's why, darling, it's incredible
> That someone so unforgettable
> Thinks that I am unforgettable too
>
> Unforgettable in every way
> And forevermore, that's how you'll stay
> That's why, darling, it's incredible
> That someone so unforgettable
> Thinks that I am unforgettable too
>
> ~ Nat King Cole
> *Lyrics by Coral Gordon & Phil Ramacon*

Help us spread the word: Yes! There is Hope!

I believe that what we're doing in teaching men and women new, old-fashioned ways for them to engage in the beautiful Dance of Romance is important work, but I need your help. Send me your feedback … send me your gal … and help us spread the word that there's hope for Christian marriage in the 21st Century!

… and tell everyone that a Hopeful Romantic told you so!

Chapter 11

LEARNING TO FOLLOW

A few years ago, I asked students in my undergraduate psychology classes if – generally speaking – they thought it would be acceptable behavior for a girl to ask a boy out on a date. The women said yes ... and so did the men ... sort of.

Further discussion revealed that, although they would find it flattering that a girl was interested in them, almost all the men said they'd feel at least a little uncomfortable with that ... and they'd rather be the one to do the asking. Go figure.

Without a doubt, women can be a great leaders. However, Romance is not the best place to demonstrate those abilities. Instead, this is the one place in the world where we get to relax and enjoy ... for the most part.

Being in relationship with a member of the opposite sex is challenging ... and hard work. And the benefits of loving a godly man by far outweigh the effort it takes to understand him. As a Hopeful Romantic, I believe that having someone to love who actually loves you back is worth more than anything else we will ever have or do in this life.

Submission in the 21st Century

Submission gets a bum rap. But it's not at all like it sounds. Submission is simply Trust and Respect. It goes like this ...

- Demonstrate unparalleled respect for him as a man.
- Trust him – and the Lord – to lead you.
- Love him just as he is.
- Long for all the best of what God has for him.
- Make him look good to others.
- And give him immediate affirmation whenever you believe he's on the right track.

As you pray for him – and I believe this should happen continually (1 Thessalonians 5:17) – it will be very helpful for you to keep these particular verses in mind:

He who finds a wife finds what is good
and receives favor from the lord. ~ Proverbs 18:22

She brings him good, not harm,
all the days of her life. ~ Proverbs 31:12

The Benefits of Partnering With a Godly Man

Always remember that you were created for him, not the other way around. Yes, I know this isn't a very popular statement, but I firmly believe it's a Fact of Life. Men don't do well without us (Genesis 2).

But when you try to turn a man into what you want him to be ... as though he were created for your benefit ... nothing good will come of it. I've never seen a situation wherein the woman called all the shots, and the relationship was a lasting and happy one for both partners.

Yes, he needs to listen to you. But if he does everything you tell him to do, you've got a serious problem on your hands.

However, you'll reap immeasurable benefits as you become the wife he needs you to be.

What more could a girl ask for than this?

- You'll be positively, absolutely irresistible to him.
- He'll joyfully protect you and provide for you, hold you and guide you.
- He'll believe in you and be Your Biggest Fan.
- He'll be proud of you when you do well, and right there for you when you need him.
- He'll love you, care for you, and respect you.

Ella Fitzgerald sang it well …

I've got a guy
Doesn't have any money
But to me he's a honey
For he's mine
And I think he's too divine

I've got a guy
When he starts into pet me
He can thrill and upset me
He's the kind that you
can't keep off you mind

I've got a guy
And he's tough
He's just a gem in the rough
But when I polish him up
I swear, he'll be a Tiffany solitaire

I'm riding high
And I'm happy and carefree
There is nothing can scare me
Cause I've got a guy

Chapter 12
WHERE DO WE GO FROM HERE?

Thank you for allowing me to share my story and passion with you. This book – like my life – is most certainly a work in progress. I don't know what the future holds. However, if past behavior is, indeed, the best predictor of future behavior, I seem destined to live out my the rest of my days as a Hopeful Romantic ... and a dancer.

And as long as the Lord is willing ... and the creek don't rise (James 4:13-16) ... that is, for as long as possible, I plan to continue to write and speak about my passion for helping Christian couples and single adults figure out better ways to apply biblical principles and the findings of scientific research to everyday life.

Remember that if you're struggling in your relationship right now, I have a pretty good idea what it feels like to be where you are. I've been there myself. And I didn't always have the support I needed. Neither of us did.

As a woman, I get where you gals are coming from. Sometimes, we can be amazingly direct in asking for what we want. At other times, we're not sure what we want. So we can also be pretty vague. Most of us have a hard time getting the men we love to understand us. It often feels like they're just trying to fix us. So, naturally, I speak "female."

As the mother of three sons, I've spent a lot of time studying the male experience. It's been a joy to watch my boys grow into men, marry, and become parents themselves. They've taught me a lot, and I'm still learning from them.

I've also studied the "Psychology Men and Traditional Masculinity" at the graduate and post-doctoral levels, and I've taught a university class on this very popular subject. What I've learned is that most women don't have a clue about men's experience, and that most men don't know how to explain it. So I've also learned to speak "male."

I've written a lot over the years. And I continue to post my thoughts online, so you can follow me if you like …

www.OCChristianCouples.com
www.Twitter.com/OCChristian
www.Facebook.com/OCChristianCounseling

I think I've got some things right. But I also realize the likelihood that some of what I "know" will change over time as I learn and grow. And that's okay. At the risk of sounding repeatedly redundant, I propose that we must all admit that we are – each one of us – still a work in progress.

… In fact, I'm already thinking of new stuff I want to share with you … and beginning to anticipate the need to write my fourth book about relationships …

The Lord is still actively at work in my life – continually showing me Wonderful Things!

What a Totally Amazing Adventure I'm on! And the most unexpected thing – the Biggest Surprise of All – occurred during this past year. I've had the blessed opportunity to learn – not only from watching other couples, but also from personal experience – that there's nothing more delightful than dancing with a perfect partner. Yes, I'm just a girl who loves the experience and the unforgettable joy of following a godly man who knows how to lead gently and confidently.

In fact, I could write a book ...

> If they asked me I could write a book
> About the way you walk and whisper and look
> I could write the preface on how we met
> So the world would never forget
>
> And the simple secret of the plot
> Is just to tell them that I love you a lot
> Then the world discovers as my book ends
> How to make two lovers of friends

~ *Lorenz Hart & Richard Rodgers*

Always the Best of Friends

I believe you should marry someone who has become your Best Friend. And if you didn't, don't worry. There's still time for you to *become* the Best of Friends!

Whether you're married, engaged, dating, or best friends, always pray for one another ...

If you're a man, wake up everyday praying: "Thank you, Lord, for this Beautiful Woman you have given me. Show me what to do to make her day – her life – better than ever. Teach me how to enhance Your Glory in her. Holy Spirit, please help me become the man she needs me to be."

If you're a woman, wake up everyday praying: "Thank you, Lord, for this Amazing Man you have put in my life. Show me what to do to make his day – his life – better than ever. Teach me how to enhance Your glory in him. Holy Spirit, please help me become the woman he needs me to be."

My prayer is that you will find the Truest of Delights in one another! May God richly bless you today ... and always!

Bibliography

Ainsworth, M., Blehar, M. Waters, E., & Wall, S. (1978). *Patterns of attachment: A psychological study of the Strange Situation.* Hillsdale, NJ: Lawrence Erlbaum Associates.

Allender, D. B., & Longman, T. (1995). *Intimate allies: Rediscovering God's design for marriage and becoming soul mates for life.* Wheaton, IL: Tyndale House Publishers, Inc.

Armstrong, A. A. (2003). *Keys to the kingdom.* Glendora, CA: PAX Programs, Inc.

Armstrong, A. A. (2008). *Making sense of men: A woman's guide to a lifetime of love, care and attention from all men.* Glendora, CA: PAX Programs, Inc.

Bartholomew, K., & Horowitz, L. M. (1991). Attachment styles among young adults: A test of a four-category model. *Journal of Personality and Social Psychology, 61,* 226-244.

Bergman, S. J. (1995). Men's psychological development: A relational perspective. In R. F. Levant & W. S. Pollack (Eds.), *A new psychology of men* (pp. 68-90). New York: Basic Books.

Bowlby, J. (1979). *The making and breaking of affectional bonds.* New York: Methuen.

Brody, L. R. (1993). On understanding gender differences in the expression of emotion: Gender roles, socialization, and language. In S. L. Ablon, D. Brown, E. J. Khantzian, & J. E. Mack (Eds.), *Human feelings: Explorations in affect development and meaning* (pp. 87-121). Hillsdale, NJ: Analytic Press.

Brody, L. R. (1997). Gender and emotion: Beyond stereotypes. *Journal of Social Issues, 53,* 369-394. Retrieved May 18, 2002, from ProQuest Research Library database.

Brody, L. R. (2000). The socialization of gender differences in emotional expression: Display rules, infant temperament, and differentiation. In A. H. Fischer (Ed.), *Gender and emotion: Social psychological perspectives* (pp. 24-47). New York: Cambridge University Press.

Brody, L. R., & Hall, J. A. (1993). Gender and emotion. In M. Lewis & J. M. Haviland (Eds.), *Handbook of emotions* (pp. 447-460). New York: Guilford Press.

Catt, M. C., Hemmings, T., & McBride, J. (Producers), & Kendrick, A. (Director). (2008). *Fireproof* [Motion picture]. United States of America: Sherwood Pictures.

Catt, M. C., Hemmings, T., & McBride, J. (Producers), & Kendrick, A. (Director). (2011). *Courageous* [Motion picture]. United States of America: Sherwood Pictures.

Eldredge, J. (2011). *Wild at heart revised and updated: Discovering the secret of a man's soul.* Nashville, TN: Thomas Nelson Publishers.

Erre, M. (2011). *Marriage* [Podcast]. Irvine, CA: Mariners Church. http://www.drdebismith.com/ephesians_5.html

Gottman, J. (1999). *The seven principles for making marriage work.* New York: Crown Publishing Group.

Greenson, R. R. (1968). Dis-identifying from mother: Its special importance for the boy. *International Journal of Psycho-Analysis, 49,* 370-374.

Gurian, M. (1994). *Mothers, sons, and lovers: How a man's relationship with his mother affects the rest of his life.* Boston: Shambhala Publications, Inc.

Gurian, M. (1996). *The wonder of boys: What parents, mentors, and educators can do to shape boys into exceptional men.* New York: Jeremy P. Tarcher/Putnam.

Hazan, C., & Shaver, P. (1987). Romantic love conceptualized as an attachment process. *Journal of Personality and Social Psychology, 52,* 511-524.

Johnson, B. (Producer), & Crowe, D. (Director). (1996). *Jerry Maguire* [Motion picture]. United States of America: Sony/Columbia.

Johnson, S. (2008). *Hold me tight: Seven conversations for a lifetime of love.* New York: Little, Brown, and Company.

Karen, R. (1998). *Becoming attached: First relationships and how they shape our capacity to love.* New York: Oxford University Press.

Levinson, D. J. (1986). *The seasons of a man's life.* New York: Ballentine Books.

Locke, H. J., & Wallace, K. M. (1959). Short marital-adjustment and prediction tests: Their reliability and validity. *Marriage and Family Living, 21,* pp. 251-255.

MacDonald, G. (1996). *When men think private thoughts: Exploring issues that captivate the minds of men.* Nashville, TN: Thomas Nelson Publishers.

Morris, G. (2012). *Men: The simpler sex?* Retrieved September 15, 2012, from http://www.net-burst.net/love/men.htm

Pollack, S. (Producer), & Lee, A. (Director). (1995). *Sense and sensibility* [Motion picture]. United States of America: Columbia Pictures.

Pollack, W. S. (1998). *Real boys: Rescuing our sons form the myths of boyhood.* New York: Henry Holt and Company.

Salkind, I. (Producer), & Donner, R. (Director). (1978). *Superman: The movie* [Motion picture]. United States of America: Warner Bros.

Smith, D. L. (2009). *Mothers and sons: How the maternal attachment experience affects boys' emotional and social development.* Garden Grove, CA: OC Christian Counseling.

Smith, D. L. (2009). *Why won't he talk to me? The simple truth about men and intimate communication.* Garden Grove, CA: OC Christian Counseling.

Also by Dr. Debi Smith

Mothers and Sons: How the Maternal Attachment
Experience Affects Boys' Emotional and Social Development

Why Won't He Talk to Me?
The Simple Truth About Men and Intimate Communication

Available for download at www.Smashwords.com

Connect With Dr. Debi Smith Online:

www.DrDebiSmith.com
Twitter.com/OCChristian
Facebook.com/OCChristianCounseling
YouTube.com/user/DrDebiSmith
www.OCChristianCounseling.com
www.OCChristianCouples.com

Made in the USA
Charleston, SC
28 September 2013